UNBLOCKING ORGANIZATIONAL VALUES

UNBLOCKING ORGANIZATIONAL VALUES

Dave Francis
Mike Woodcock

In Association with
University Associates, Inc.
San Diego, California

Scott, Foresman and Company
Glenview, Illinois   London

Library of Congress Cataloging-in-Publication Data

Francis, Dave.
 Unblocking organizational values / Dave Francis and Mike Woodcock.
 p.   cm.
 "In association with University Associates, Inc., San Diego,
California."
 Includes index.
 ISBN 0-673-38917-0
 1. Corporate culture. 2. Organizational effectiveness.
I. Woodcock, Mike. II. Title.
HD58.7.F697   1990
658.4 — dc20   89-10248
                                                       CIP

1 2 3 4 5 6 MUR 94 93 92 91 90 89

ISBN 0-673-38917-0

Scott, Foresman professional books are available for bulk sales at quantity discounts.
For information, please contact Marketing Manager, Professional Books Group, Scott,
Foresman and Company, 1900 East Lake Avenue, Glenview, IL 60025.

Contents

Introduction: Something Old, Something New, Something Borrowed, Something Blue

We know what you are thinking: this is a crazy title for the introduction to a book on management. Maybe not. Let us explain.

This book argues that managers in successful commercial organizations hold roughly similar sets of values, and that successful managers have thought deeply about their own beliefs and then aligned their organization's values with those values described in this book.

The time-honored advice given to a new bride captures the essential points. Successful management is a marriage of tried and tested values (something old), visionary thinking (something new), techniques gathered from other successful enterprises (something borrowed), and an enduring concern with achievement (something blue — the color of the Conservative Party in the United Kingdom, where we both live).

A *value* is a belief in action. It is a choice about what is good or bad, important or unimportant. Values shape behavior. Until a value is acted upon it remains an aspiration. Values are hard to detect; yet they underpin organizations like the foundations of a house. If the foundation is weak, then the house falls down.

Every organization has a system of values, whether that fact is realized or not. The most important value systems are located in the management group—especially at the top. Those who occupy directing roles must have an active value system—this is what top leadership is all about. In practice the principle extends right down the hierarchy; all managers make decisions of principle that profoundly influence the part of the community which they govern.

From this point of view, management is a form of politics—the use of power in pursuit of collective aims. Managers establish systems for law-making, investment, justice, motivation, defense, and so on. The ways that this power is used define the historical and cultural identity of organizations.

Because those who shape the destiny of organizations usually have strong personalities, their views really matter. What do these people believe in? This book is an answer to that vital question.

Unblocking Organizational Values is a practical guide to value clarification for managers. It is intended for four audiences:

- Managers who want to develop their own capability
- Management teams who want to survey the values in their own organization
- Personnel managers and consultants who design organization development programs
- Students of management who will one day be in positions of power

This last category, students of management, deserves special mention. Very few courses for the master of business administration degree contain a program on values. It was not until 1987 that the Harvard Business School received a grant to establish a course which examines the ethical implications of management decision-making. We believe that much more attention needs to be paid to the topic. Aspiring managers, who will shortly be in positions of power, need to have clarified their own values and thought about the implications of their stances on matters of principle.

At this point the authors wish to state frankly that there is no scientific process by which the ingredients for management success can be identified. Management is a *craft* in the medieval sense of the word. It is based on beliefs which are implemented by instruction, practice, first-hand knowledge, and close attention to detail.

To define the foundations of the craft of management, the authors undertook a four-year study of interview, observation, and "measurement" using the Organizational Values Questionnaire which is reproduced in Chapter 2. We sifted through our observations and data to detect significant patterns.

First we needed a definition of *success*. For commercial organizations the task was relatively easy—sustained financial success is the only criterion which can be used. In noncommercial organizations the definition of success is more blurred. How do you measure the performance of a prison or a hospital? We took critical acclaim by informed observers as our criterion here.

Fortunately the authors were well placed to make the analysis. Our work enabled us to become "participant observers." Dave Francis is a consultant on organization strategy and development. His close association with major international companies provided much detailed observation of values in action. A member of Parliament, Mike Woodcock has been a member of both the House of Commons Select Committees on Trade and Industry and Home Affairs and has had the opportunity to review many case studies not only in Britain and many European countries, but also in Turkey, China, Indonesia, Thailand, Tanzania, and South Africa. Together we visited organizations in countries as far apart as Sweden and Mexico, Spain and India, New Zealand and the United States.

As we debated the patterns which emerged from the data, we were struck by the similarity of managerial values across cultures, even in the communist bloc. In commercial organizations, those managements that were successful, not surprisingly, had an almost total preoccupation with profitability. But there was another subtle theme which we called "the concern with legacy." This meant that successful managers were striving to build something worthwhile to pass on to the next generation. These managers knew that mere wealth creation was insufficient to inspire most people and to sustain their hopes. They created organizations with a heart as well as a pocket.

Successful noncommercial organizations replaced the ethic of profitability with a deeply understood, but continually evolving, notion of "contribution." Their leaders had exhaustively examined the options (including the needs of their environments) and come to a firm decision about their corporate identity. Managers in great hospitals, theaters, prisons, or universities know their mission with total clarity — which has a concept of the organization's contribution at the core.

Managers have often been cast in the role of harsh, reactionary exploiters. Listening to those who hold such crude stereotyped views, one could be forgiven for believing that most managers are unenlightened and uncaring individuals. This is often the opposite of the truth. We found that, at its best, management is profound, positive, relevant to today's needs, and deeply humanitarian at its core.

So, in part, this is a book about management morality. The authors do not pretend that management always equals good, and we acknowledge that some managers have adopted exploitative, damaging, and self-aggrandizing strategies to the detriment of those whom they manage and many others.

Successful managements establish what people really want and shape an organization to fill a void. They provide opportunities to help their employees to thrive and develop. Management, at its best, is based on a mature insight of what is, not an idealistic concept of what might be.

We devoted years to completing this book, which provides a framework for managers, especially those near the top, to review their organization's values in the hope that some beneficial change may be stimulated. We believe that successful managerial philosophies are based on fundamentally decent values; otherwise, the right to manage is not earned.

In periods of rapid change or confusion, people need a rock to stand on. This gives the confidence to enter the unknown and effectively manage change. A strong set of beliefs and values, shared by the management cadre, provides the necessary foundation for coping with difficulty. Hence, it is important that managers know the prevailing values which guide behavior in their organizations and change those which are negative or destructive.

The topic of management culture has been much discussed, but the crucial importance of values has been insufficiently realized. Values in organizations are mainly established and maintained by leaders. Most people in organizations look to the top for a definition of what is important. We need "heros" at the apex of organizations and "mini-heros" in all sections of the management structure. Values are essential whenever decisions are made, goals are set, or problems are solved. This is not moralistic: it happens anyway. All people in positions of power are advised to clarify and test their values.

As authors, we acknowledge a considerable debt to others who have analyzed and discussed management sciences. In particular, the work of Maury Smith on value clarification and Henry Mintzberg on organizations have been great inspirations. There is, of course, no implication that either of these authors, or any of the other writers quoted in the text, agree with the thesis expressed here. Our chief debt, of course, is to the hundreds of managers who have answered our questions and helped us to clarify our thinking.

Dave Francis
Mike Woodcock

London, United Kingdom

PART ONE

Basics

CHAPTER 1

The Development of Management Values

THE PARABLE OF THE CHINESE PRISON

A visitor to China went to see a prison on the outskirts of Canton. Entering the heavy gates of the stark building, he expected to observe an oppressive regime with men incarcerated in almost medieval conditions. Exactly the opposite was the case. The prison was humming with purposeful activity. An orchestra consisting of felons and murderers was practicing a Mozart piece. Forgers and pimps were learning poetry. In every quarter there was a spirit of "improvement."

The visitor interviewed the prison governor, who said, "Our mission is to awaken the good in wrongdoers. This is not a prison in the accepted sense. We aim to be a true reformatory."

A prison, like any other organization, is an institution built on a foundation of values. If the Canton prison governor had seen his task as merely custodial, then everything would have been different. There would have been no indoctrination, culture, or education. The emphasis would have been on constant surveillance and unpickable locks.

Just to remind you, values are "beliefs about what is good or bad, important or not important." Values beget attitudes which specify behavior. The values of those who hold power fundamentally shape the character of an organization.

Ideally, all those who hold powerful roles within an organization share the same basic values. Think about the Chinese prison again. What would have happened if the prison governor had adopted enlightened values while at the same time the staff were repressive toward the prisoners? There are three possibilities: The governor might succeed in changing the values of his staff; he might force compliance; or the staff might undermine the governor's power.

Since the effective power in an organization is spread across management — and sometimes wider — our research clearly shows that successful managements achieve a vital consensus on basic values. (Our definition of *success* is stated in the Introduction.) Without a shared understanding of mission, an organization is in peril of being figuratively, and perhaps literally, torn apart.

How is this consensus achieved? Values arise from leaders. However, there is a more subtle influence. Those in positions of power are influenced by the spirit of the times. Managers look outside themselves for guidance, whether they recognize it or not.

Values should be related to a particular context. Parents must look at the choices they make when rearing children; doctors must examine questions of medical ethics; and managers must examine the specific issues related to the task of governing productive communities. Where should we begin our search for those managerial values which spell success?

This chapter follows the path that the authors took when they began their study of managerial values, examining the development of management ideology in the twentieth century. Each era had something to offer. An assessment of the evolutions and revolutions in management values is a useful basis for this study. The chapter concludes by selecting the key themes of each phase and defining its enduring value. As you read the next few pages, try to assess which era of management values has most affected your own thinking.

Much has been written about the art and science of getting things done through people. There are an increasing number of sources of indoctrination that shape the minds of leaders. Auto-biographies of management heroes adorn airport bookstalls and are avidly read by occupants of aircraft club-class seats. New managers go to business school to learn their trade. The resources of mass media are being used. For example, in Great Britain an increasing amount of management guidance is given on television through the "Open Business School." There is a whole industry devoted to satisfying the hunger of managers for inspiration and guidance. The effect of this "propaganda" is partly to standardize the intellectual activity of managers.

Why is this trend important? We believe that there are influences on the values of managers that have actually under-mined organizational effectiveness. Successful managers discrim-inate as to their sources of influence. In other words, managers are unwise if they unquestioningly accept the viewpoints of today's pundit. Leaders must avoid trendy fashions and answer basic questions for themselves. Each era of management thinking has made a significant contribution. The lesson is obvious: managements must capture the best of each evolutionary phase and develop their own composite philosophy.

Management is a twentieth-century craft. When viewing from a historical perspective, we see that there has been considerable change in the influences which have shaped the values of western managers. Only in the last ninety years has the role of the *manager* become distinct, with an accompanying development of values.

There are seven key evolutionary stages in the development of management values. The first stage of values to dominate management thinking was that a person should be treated as a perfectible machine who is motivated by material gain. These values were based on basic concepts of organization that were first analyzed approximately one hundred years ago. It was Max Weber who described the concepts of authority, hierarchy, roles, and formalized procedures. Such organizational devices enable human machines, or "bureaucracies," to be devised to perform complex but repetitive tasks.

In the first half of the twentieth century, as organizations grew, they became overwhelmingly concerned with efficiency. Scientific thinking accelerated the pace of change. Mass production methods changed the working lives of millions of people. Slowly the fruits of improved organizations were harvested, and material comforts became more available.

It was found that people were more efficient when their work was carefully programmed. A new profession, work-study engineering, developed. People with clipboards and stop watches began to observe workers and to make changes in routines. The incremental effect was a massive improvement in productivity through meticulous analytical techniques that improved performance through careful experiment, specification of standards, and training. Most leadership advice of the time was based on values which assumed that men and women are a resource like any other and that they are machines motivated solely by money. The prevailing philosophy is best summed up in the writings of Frederick William Taylor, the "father of work study," who advocated the obsessive pursuit of rationality in every aspect of life.

Such mechanistic techniques made possible the management of large enterprises. Workers found themselves performing routine work alongside millions of others—but all was not well. New research studies (such as at the Hawthorn Plant in the United States) demonstrated that nonrational factors like feelings and attitudes profoundly influenced behavior and performance.

A second era of management values began. Progressive managers adopted a more complex view of the human being, realizing that feelings and willpower played a significant and sometimes crucial role in influencing productivity. Experiments were introduced to try to improve the individual's attitudes at work. Supervisors were trained to be team leaders, and new techniques for motivation were instituted. The new human relations school refused to accept the assumptions of the school of mechanistic management.

After World War II a new situation effected a revolutionary change in the power structure of organizations. The third revolution in organizational values was not created by management — it was instead a response to the rise of trade union power. Management was forced to learn to fight. In the 1950s there was a great shortage of products and labor; almost everything that could be made could be sold, so apparently there was little to be gained from being outstandingly creative or efficient. Trade unions gained in power because larger organizations could be held for ransom by the disruption of a few key workers. Values rooted in preindustrial agricultural life, such as diligence, opportunism, and a "fair day's work for a fair day's pay," were derided — especially in the older industrial nations like Britain.

Many managements invested enormous amounts of effort in containing unrest and keeping peace. The values of the era were adversarial, with shifts from confrontation to conciliation depending on management's view of the politics of the situation. It was questionable who was in charge of organizational values as active trade union leaders made so much of the running.

From the early 1960s, as the western world recovered from the shortages created by World War II, many commercial companies encountered increasing difficulty in maintaining their profitability and market share. How could the problems of low efficiency, poor motivation, stagnant innovation, and reactionary trade unionism be tackled? Various approaches were tried, including the disastrous philosophy of lowering the quality of the product. Britain in particular seemed to be on a relentless downward spiral, losing the commitment to the values which had made her strong. Ironically, managements perceived people both as a valuable resource and as the biggest barrier to change. In many cases, managements came to believe that head-to-head confrontation was the worst available option and therefore sought new ways of solving power problems. Slowly an answer appeared: democracy in the workplace.

Gradually, a fourth phase of managerial values became fashionable. This was the ideology of workplace democracy that challenged long-held management beliefs. The boss was no longer the boss. In the need for a new armory of techniques, American influences began to play a dominant role. In 1960 Douglas McGregor published *The Human Side of Enterprise*,[1] a book destined to have a profound impact on management thinking across the world. McGregor spelled out the importance of management value systems by dividing the beliefs into two opposite stances that he called Theory X and Theory Y. Theory X managers believe that people are naturally deceitful, lazy, and motivated primarily by their self interest, therefore requiring tight supervision and financial rewards. On the other hand, Theory Y managers believe that people are naturally positive, trustworthy, altruistic, and constructive. McGregor argues that these two stances are self-fulfilling prophesies: if people are managed by a Theory X viewpoint, they will be uncooperative and deceitful; whereas if people are managed by a Theory Y viewpoint, they will be positive and self-motivated.

Many managers tried to develop a Theory Y style, but were unwilling to go the whole hog. One senior manager reflected, "We tried to trust people but never really took it seriously. So we diminished our Theory X behavior and replaced this with a wishy-washy participative style which proved disastrous for all concerned."

However, organizational idealism paralleled the mood of liberation and heady excitement of the 1960s. In almost every area of life, people experimented with new ways of living, wanting to break the shackles of the past and to plunge into the unknown. It was a time when everything was questioned, and authority was portrayed as outmoded and repressive. The concept of "Flower Power" and the Beatles' song "All You Need Is Love" typified the spirit of the times.

This phase of the development of management ideology was very confusing. Supervisors whose task was to ensure that ten thousand switches were made every hour were also required to help machine operators achieve a state of "self-actualization." Managers who felt that they needed structure, predictability, and performance were told to be radical and libertarian, and to "hang loose." This situation could not last; the values of California hippies were unsuited to running productive enterprises.

The response was a new era of management values. The fifth era was "management by objectives." Each person should have comprehensive, agreed-upon output targets but allowed the freedom to determine the means of achievement. The aim was to harmonize the needs of the organization with the needs of the individual. Although the principle was sound, managers found that MBO was suitable only in relatively stable environments, and even then it produced red tape.

Managers became disenchanted with MBO, realizing that the technique was not the organizational philosophers' stone. A new set of management values became current — the sixth phase. The managers of the 1970s increasingly turned to the mushrooming field of applied behavioral science for their mentors. In that setting occurred the remarkable spectacle of senior managers attentively listening to gurus whose expertise was radical psychotherapy. Many of the new authorities were American academics who had gained experience in the sunrise industries such as space science and high technology. As fads in management thinking emerged, managers began to ask "What is the flavor of the month?' With hindsight, it is easy to see that many managers tried to implement fashionable new beliefs with only a superficial understanding.

An analysis of the management propaganda of this era shows a distinct antiauthority bias. As the role of the manager was being questioned, the concept of facilitator was advocated. Grand schemes for overhauling corporations were devised under the banner of "organization development." Managerial philosophers propounded a total social-engineering approach based on utopian humanistic values.

Many managements that wanted to use progressive techniques wholeheartedly embraced organization development. Top managers liked the notion that it is possible systematically to change organizational culture and processes. Enormous sums of money were spent in those heady years on schemes that were later evaluated as failures. Only a few of those grandiose schemes survived into the 1980s, and they have been carefully integrated into line management. Those same outside experts who used to rule the roost have been demoted to their proper role as advisers.

Part of the organization development phase was an explosive growth of self-development activities. For example, experimental groups in self-understanding, known as T-groups, were instituted. Managers were put in unstructured situations, often in remote locations, with a gurulike figure whose guidance was "We will learn from what happens." Behavioral scientists had discovered that people learn more when the structures which support their present attitudes and perceptions are taken away. Many managers — over 50 percent — reported that although the T-group experience was profound and valuable, an increasing awareness of negative psychological side effects contributed to such training techniques falling into disrepute. The aim was right: managers need to be aware of who they are and what impact they make on others. Unfortunately the techniques were often used by underqualified trainers. One manager, reviewing this era, commented, "Navel-gazing replaced discipline, and self-expression ruled the roost. It was a dangerous fashion."

Self-development activities blossomed in the 1970s. The work of psychotherapists became fashionable. Perhaps the most influential was Eric Berne, who developed a technique called transactional analysis which interpreted the exchanges (transactions) between people. Berne's work took managers on a fascinating voyage of self-discovery that enabled them to relate their insights to their management role. In particular, Berne helped many managers to see that they played destructive interpersonal games which sustained a negative emotional climate. Improved emotional health became an objective for many managers. Transactional analysis brought alive truths in a way that no other popular approach to psychology had done. However, examine the other side of the coin for a moment. Studying psychotherapies can result in a temptation to dilute self-expression with understanding.

For example, a drive for achievement can be interpreted as a manifestation of a neurotic personality. Creativity becomes expressed through human relationships rather than in the achievement of business objectives. As one observer noticed, "The eye is taken off the ball when psychology becomes king." A half-submerged assumption that people ought always to be nice to each other blunts the cut and thrust of debate. Interactions become games to be analyzed rather than the action of getting on with the job. There is no more irritating person in management circles than a transactional-analysis freak who is more concerned with expressing "warm fuzzies" than achieving results.

Part of the sixth phase of the development of management thought was a growing concern with the quality of working life. Managers began analyzing the dehumanizing and stressful aspects of organizational life. Fred Hertzberg, an American professor, made a major impact on the minds of managers in the 1970s. With refreshing candor, he probed into job satisfaction and motivation. Hertzberg concluded that material reward, supervision, and physical environment did little to provide positive motivation. There was a great need to build the opportunity for achievement into the very structure of the job. Unfortunately, it proved very difficult to find ways of enriching jobs to provide sustained challenge. People began to feel that they were "entitled" to be satisfied at work. In some companies the efforts that management made to improve the quality of work life, ironically, provoked bitterness as it proved impossible to meet the early promises made to employees. The sense of detachment is summarized in a poem of the era (found on a café wall in Twickenham, England).

Work

If you work and do your best
You'll get the sack like all the rest,
But if you laze and sod about
You'll live to see the job right out
The work is hard, the pay is small
So take your time and sod them all.

The techniques we have mentioned—organization development, T-groups, transactional analysis, and quality of working life programs—are examples of the prevalent managerial values in the 1970s. The themes of involvement and participation were based on an underlying belief that people would support that in which they felt personally involved. Expectations were raised. Many people felt that they should not only participate in decisions but also have the power of veto. Sometimes labyrinthine participative structures were established to provide the means of participation.

Despite such optimistic theories and brave experiments, participation and involvement proved inadequate weapons in the fight against enterprise in the Far East. Somehow, such countries as Japan, which had been written off as poor performers, were trouncing the West. As a result, it became necessary to make harsh decisions, and so the seventh phase of management thinking was rather brutally born.

This last phase in the development of management ideology is interesting because it was reactionary rather than progressive. By the end of the 1970s, managers began to rediscover lessons which their organizational grandparents knew well. Such themes as "nothing for free," "hard work leads to success," and "the customer is always right" began to be heard again. This was most obvious in Britain where the political stance of Margaret Thatcher's government, first elected in 1979, explicitly encouraged the virtues of Victorian values. Power battles were fought against trade unions—with the establishment determined to win. The motivational power of individual opportunism, ownership, and self-responsibility (all nineteenth-century values) were rediscovered. Attempts to democratize commercial organizations were reversed. State ownership decreased in France, Japan, Australia, New Zealand, Great Britain, and many other countries. Managements in the Western world moved towards the political right in step with the governments of the day.

The seventh phase is a synthesis of the previous stages. After decades of drifting, managers have recognized that they have the tough task of leading, controlling, and winning. Now, with global competition, there are many more threats. Only the fittest will survive.

SUCCESSFUL VALUES

Where do we look for the values which increase the probability that a management group will be successful? Beginning with the preceding analysis, the authors found that the following key themes occur:

Stage	Theme	Enduring Value
1st	Rationality	Scientific Analysis Pays
2nd	Emotionality	Care for People Pays
3rd	Confrontation	Strong Defense Is Vital
4th	Consensus	Politics Matters
5th	Organization/Individual Balance	Performance Is King
6th	Potential	People Can Develop
7th	Realism	Nothing Good Comes Easily

   This information provided a basis for the practical study of managerial values. In the next chapter, you will undertake a study of the values in your own organization. Only then, to avoid prejudicing you, will we tell you the results of our research.

REFERENCES

1. McGregor, D. (1960). *The Human Side of Enterprise*. New York: McGraw-Hill.

PART TWO

Measurement

The Organizational Values Questionnaire

If you accept the idea that values are the foundation of the character of an organization, then it follows that managers must strive to adopt a system of values that promotes success. Now it's time for you to do some work! Before delving further into this book, you should take stock of the values which operate in your organization. This analysis will relate the conceptual model of this book to your own situation.

On page 19 you will find the Organizational Values Questionnaire. This may be completed by one individual or may be used as a survey of the views of many people within an organization. However, the Organizational Values Questionnaire is used only with managerial, supervisory, and professional staff.

Complete the questionnaire now. Instructions for interpretation follow.

ORGANIZATIONAL VALUES QUESTIONNAIRE

This questionnaire asks your opinions about a specific organization, or part of an organization. It may be a site, department, company, branch, or an entire organization. Before you begin, define the unit that you wish to study and write an unmistakable definition in the box below. (When several people complete the survey together, they should ensure that they are all using the same definition of the unit being assessed.)

The unit being assessed is _____

Answer the sixty items below *only* in relation to this definition of the unit. Please give your opinion on each item. Even if you do not have enough information to make a definitive judgment, answer to the best of your knowledge. Allocate points as shown.

The statement is

Totally true	4 points
Largely true	3 points
Neither true nor false	2 points
Largely untrue	1 point
Totally untrue	0 points

Questionnaire

The sixty items:

1. Managers act in ways which demonstrate that they are in charge. (Score ____)

2. Much effort is invested in developing managers so that they achieve a high standard of competence. (Score ____)

3. Outstanding managerial performance is well rewarded. (Score ____)

4. Great care is taken to ensure that *key* management decisions are well considered. (Score ____)

5. There is a constant search for ways to do things more efficiently. (Score ____)

6. Managers avoid spending money unnecessarily. (Score ____)

7. People with genuine difficulties are treated with compassion by management. (Score ____)

8. Care is taken to ensure that everyone feels part of a team. (Score ____)

9. Organizational rules and regulations are considered to be fair. (Score ____)

10. The organization is aggressive in defense of its own interests. (Score ____)

11. Everyone is aware of the importance of care for the customer. (Score ____)

12. Innovation and creativity are encouraged. (Score ____)

13. Management is respected. (Score ____)

14. Considerable efforts are made to appoint the best candidates to management positions. (Score ____)

15. Managers receive regular feedback on how they are performing.   (Score ____)

16. Over the past few years, the strategic decisions taken by top management have proved largely successful.
                                    (Score ____)

17. New technologies and techniques are regularly investigated to see whether they could increase efficiency.
                                    (Score ____)

18. Great efforts are made to ensure that people understand the economic contribution they are making.   (Score ____)

19. Employees are always given a fair hearing when disputes arise.   (Score ____)

20. Teambuilding techniques are used appropriately.   (Score ____)

21. Justice is done and seen to be done.   (Score ____)

22. Threats to the organization are treated seriously.
                                    (Score ____)

23. This is an organization that believes in "being competitive with the best."   (Score ____)

24. New ideas are highly valued.   (Score ____)

25. Managers are widely perceived to have earned the authority which they exercise.   (Score ____)

26. Great efforts are made to develop the skills of managers.
                                    (Score ____)

27. Managerial rewards are clearly linked to performance.
                                    (Score ____)

28. Top managers plan well for the future.   (Score ____)

29. The organization is renowned for high quality goods or services.   (Score ____)

30. Managers are appraised on the cost-effectiveness of their units.   (Score ____)

31. Top managers demonstrate by their actions that they care about the well-being of the people in the organization.

(Score ____)

32. Employees strongly identify with their work unit.

(Score ____)

33. Basic codes of conduct are well understood.　(Score ____)

34. Trade unions do not undermine the well-being of the organization.

(Score ____)

35. Competition between work groups is utilized to raise standards of performance.

(Score ____)

36. The organization seizes opportunities as they occur.

(Score ____)

37. Those with responsibilities are given commensurate authority.

(Score ____)

38. People with management potential get real opportunities to develop their careers.

(Score ____)

39. Performance is the main criterion by which managers are evaluated.

(Score ____)

40. Top management decisions are communicated effectively.

(Score ____)

41. Low standards are not tolerated in this organization.

(Score ____)

42. Managers demonstrate by their actions that they understand the "laws of the marketplace."　(Score ____)

43. This organization is considered to be a good employer.

(Score ____)

44. This is an organization in which people go out of their way to be helpful to each other.　(Score ____)

45. Internal rules and regulations are fair.　(Score ____)

46. Management deals effectively with anything or anyone that could inhibit success.

(Score ____)

47. Destructive competition between departments is avoided.

(Score ____)

48. Entrepreneurial skills are highly valued.   (Score ____)

49. Managers keep the organization "on course." (Score ____)

50. The performance of managers is regularly evaluated.

(Score ____)

51. People get rewarded for doing things that enable the organization to be successful.   (Score ____)

52. Managers have been well trained in decision-making techniques.   (Score ____)

53. Pride in the job is demonstrated at all levels.

(Score ____)

54. Financial resources are used prudently.   (Score ____)

55. There are no destructive class or racial barriers in this organization.   (Score ____)

56. Deliberate steps are taken to develop effective teamwork throughout the organization.   (Score ____)

57. Rules help, rather than hinder, work accomplishment.

(Score ____)

58. Management fights to protect the organization's interests.

(Score ____)

59. Competitiveness in relation to other companies is regularly measured.   (Score ____)

60. Good ideas get acted upon quickly.   (Score ____)

Answer Sheet

Write your score against each item number, and then total the horizontal columns.

TOTALS

1	13	25	37	49		Power: managers must manage
2	14	26	38	50		Elitism: 'Cream at the Top'
3	15	27	39	51		Reward: performance is king
4	16	28	40	52		Effectiveness: doing the right things
5	17	29	41	53		Efficiency: doing things right
6	18	30	42	54		Economy: no free lunches
7	19	31	43	55		Fairness: who cares wins
8	20	32	44	56		Teamwork: pulling together
9	21	33	45	57		Law and Order: justice must prevail
10	22	34	46	58		Defense: know thine enemy
11	23	35	47	59		Competitiveness: survival of the fittest
12	24	36	48	60		Opportunism: who dares wins

Interpreting the Questionnaire

You have now scored the questionnaire and are no doubt wondering what it means.

You have a score for each of the twelve organizational values identified on the right-hand side of the answer sheet. High scores indicate a strong value, low scores suggest a weakness!

In the next chapter we show how the twelve values fit together into a comprehensive theory. Each of the subsequent chapters takes one value and describes its importance. We argue that a sound organizational value system requires *all* twelve values to be strong.

Consider our arguments, evaluate whether you agree, and try the action ideas at the end of each chapter.

C H A P T E R 3

Twelve into Four Does Go

Now that you have completed the Organizational Values Questionnaire, you will have an idea about which are the strong and which are the weak values in your organization; but remember that one person's view is subjective and therefore should not be acted upon without further verification. However, completing the questionnaire will also make it easier to relate the theory of this book to your situation.

The answer sheet gives a score for twelve values that are vital for your commercial success. These values are derived from four core issues and twelve subissues which have to be addressed by managers. The twelve values are associated with successful management practice. Organizations that adhere to these values have the greater chance of success in today's world. In this chapter we define these values in outline and consider the process of clarifying values in an organization.

Our research and experience clearly point to the conclusion that in today's world, if an organization is to be successful, it must be able to do the following:

1. **Manage management**. The organization must deal with issues related to the power and the role of management. It must ensure that the management role is clearly defined, and that managers are capable people.
2. **Manage the task**. It must deal with the issues involved in getting the job done. Any commercial organization will fail if it does not achieve its goals.
3. **Manage relationships**. It must deal with the issues of getting the best contribution from its people. Every organization is made up of people; the job does not get done without commitment.
4. **Manage the environment**. It must deal with the issues of the competitive marketplace. It must know the environment in which it operates, and seek to influence that environment to its advantage.

Managing management, managing the task, managing relationships, and managing the environment are the four core issues leading to twelve subissues from which the twelve values are derived. These values have been derived from our research into those practices and beliefs which have shown themselves to be enduring in successful organizations. However, every organization operates in an environment which is, in some ways, unique. Additional issues may need to be addressed and other values formulated to suit a particular organization.

The four core issues, the twelve subissues, and the twelve values form an integrated system. Their potential is realized when all are addressed with vigor and consistency. Our thesis is that the foundation of successful management is the active and persistent pursuit of *all* of the twelve values reviewed by the questionnaire.

THE FIRST CORE ISSUE — MANAGING MANAGEMENT

Because almost every organization is complex, specialist functions must be integrated in order for the organization to operate. Only management can direct and coordinate the complex elements of the organization. To achieve success, the management resource must be well defined, well selected, well trained, and well motivated. We call this process "managing management."

The three subissues which need to be addressed are the following:

Power. The management group has the knowledge, authority, and position to decide the mission of the enterprise, acquire resources, and make decisions. The successful management understands the inherent power of its position and takes charge of the organization's destiny. It adopts this value: *Managers must manage.*

Elitism. The management task is complex and important. The quality of people who fill management roles is crucial. An inadequate manager can wreak havoc — both by sins of commission and by sins of omission. The successful organization understands the vital importance of getting the best possible candidates into management jobs and of continuously developing their competence. It adopts this value: *Cream belongs at the top.*

Reward. The performance of those who lead an organization is crucial. Managers need to perform consistently and energetically in pursuit of the organization's goals. The successful organization identifies and rewards success. It adopts this value: *Performance is king.*

THE SECOND CORE ISSUE — MANAGING THE TASK

Work can be dull, grueling, demanding, challenging, and worrying. In the final analysis, every organization is concerned with output, not with the toughness of the task. This concept means that "the job must be done, and done well." It requires focusing on clear objectives, working efficiently, and conserving resources. We call this process "managing the task."

The three subissues which need to be addressed are these:

> **Effectiveness.** Focusing on the right issues must be a constant concern. Unless effort is well directed, somewhere a smarter management will find ways of taking your market. A successful organization is able to focus resources on activities that get results. It adopts this value: *Do the right thing.*
>
> **Efficiency.** It has been said that good management is about doing hundreds of little things well. All too often a small error has a disproportionate effect on the quality of the whole. The drive to do everything well gives a sharp edge. The successful organization relentlessly searches for better ways to do things, and it constantly builds pride into the job. It adopts this value: *Do things right.*
>
> **Economy.** It is a great deal easier to spend money than to make it. Lack of effective cost control is a common cause of business failure and organizational waste. The discipline rendered by the profit-and-loss account endows the wise commercial enterprise with the ultimate measure of success. Every activity costs money; someone, somewhere has to pay. The successful organization understands the importance of facing economic reality. It adopts this value: *No free lunches.*

THE THIRD CORE ISSUE — MANAGING RELATIONSHIPS

Managers expect a lot from the people who work in the organization; they demand hard work, loyalty, skill, care, and honesty. Employees will give such commitments only to a management that is perceived as being fit to govern. People need to be treated with compassion, to feel valued, and to believe that rules and regulations are just. We call this process "managing relationships."

The three subissues which need to be addressed are these:

Fairness. One of the greatest compliments paid to a good teacher is that he or she is "firm but fair." Managements, by their actions, greatly affect people's lives, both in work and outside. What they do, and what they refuse to do, has a major impact on the quality of life of all employees. Using this power with compassion and fairness builds trust and commitment. The successful organization realizes that people's views, perceptions, and feelings are important. It adopts this value: *Who cares wins*.

Teamwork. A well-organized and well-motivated group can achieve more than the sum of the individuals who comprise the group. People enjoy the company of others and can work well collectively. One person's talents can balance the weaknesses of another. It is vitally important that people feel that they belong. The successful organization ensures that it derives the benefits of effective teamwork. It adopts this value: *Pulling together*.

Law and order. Every community develops a framework of laws that regulate conduct. These provide the ground rules of acceptable behavior. An organization exercises considerable power over the lives of its employees and their families, with managers operating as judge and jury, often without a right of appeal. The successful organization devises and honorably administers an appropriate system of rules and regulations. It adopts the value: *Justice must prevail.*

THE FOURTH CORE ISSUE – MANAGING THE ENVIRONMENT

Every organization exists within an environment — sometimes turbulent, often hostile and complex. The management must really understand its environment from all viewpoints — social, technical, economic, and competitive. Without this information, it is impossible to make wise decisions. In order to survive and succeed in its environment, the organization must formulate a strategy of aggressive defense to protect its interests, take all necessary steps to be competitive, and seize opportunities whenever they occur. We call this process "managing the environment."

The three subissues which need to be addressed are these:

Defense. For many organizations it is a dog-eat-dog world. In every commercial organization, there are talented people planning strategies to increase their business at the expense of the competition. Many noncommercial organizations find themselves under threat from those who provide their funds. The successful organization studies external threats and then formulates a strong defense. It adopts this value: *Know thine enemy.*

Competitiveness. The capacity to be competitive is the only surefire recipe for survival. Usually, this fact is recognized at the top level, but it is less likely that the message is understood throughout the rest of the organization. The successful organization takes all necessary steps to be competitive. It knows that in the world of commerce, it is the best who survive and the weakest who go to the wall. It adopts this value: *Survival of the fittest.*

Opportunism. Despite the most brilliant planning, it is inevitable that unexpected opportunities and threats will occur. An organization cannot afford to ignore the unexpected. It is wiser actively to seek out new opportunities than to allow others, more fleet of foot, to grab the best chances. Opportunities have to be seized quickly, even though this may involve risks. The successful organization is a committed opportunist. It adopts this value: *Who dares wins.*

The preceding values are the foundations of organizational success. Each raises issues that need to be addressed. The twelve values, we conclude, encapsulate the characteristics of high-performing organizations in today's world.

Core Issues	Subissues	Values
Managing management	Power Elitism Reward	Managers must manage. Cream belongs at the top. Performance is king.
Managing the task	Effectiveness Efficiency Economy	Do the right thing. Do things right. There are no free lunches.
Managing relationships	Fairness Teamwork Law and order	Who cares wins. Pull together. Justice must prevail.
Managing the environment	Defense Competitiveness Opportunism	Know thine enemy. Only the fittest survive. Who dares wins.

CLARIFYING VALUES

These are the twelve issues which determine success. They can also be shown as a diagram (see Figure 1).

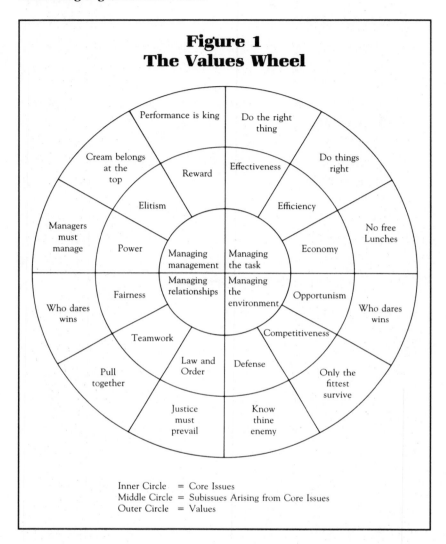

Figure 1
The Values Wheel

Inner Circle = Core Issues
Middle Circle = Subissues Arising from Core Issues
Outer Circle = Values

Our values, whether we are aware of it or not, determine our daily behavior. This is especially true for those in positions of power who must have both clear and productive values. A management is weak and unfocused without a coherent value system. Power must always be used with wisdom and subtlety — domination will always be resisted.

"Committed management" strives to do what is profitable but also what feels right. Values have to be known, consistent, practiced, and honored. Values oriented to success need constantly to be reinforced. There is no alternative. Leaders with clear values are able to attract others toward them, thereby enabling the organization to develop a consensus about what is good or bad and what is important or not important.

The process of clarifying organizational values should be undertaken systematically. Much of the information derives from the experience, beliefs, and feelings of the senior management group. Value clarification is one of the few topics in management in which inner beliefs are probably more important than external analysis.

A clarified value meets eight conditions, which are as follows:

1. *Values must be chosen from alternatives.* Only values that have been positively chosen will be firmly held, since the act of choosing strengthens commitment.

Senior management must debate issues of principle in order to choose those values which they are prepared to fight to protect. For such debates to be meaningful, managers need to consider each of the twelve issues described in this chapter. Managers should adopt a comparative approach and study successful and unsuccessful competitors to discover the values which have been shown to succeed in their own industry.

2. *Values must be consistent with each other.* Values must support each other, because values pulling in different directions are destructive.

For example, an organization may adopt the strategic driving force "we will be innovative" and yet reward managers for avoiding failure. This would be inherently contradictory; hence the message would be confused. Managers must study the "package" of values that they live by, and they should check to ensure that they are they intellectually and behaviorally consistent.

3.   Values should be limited in number. Trying to adopt an excessive number of values dissipates effort and confuses. Values are broad, deep, and general.

The four core issues we identified have been translated into twelve values, and these can provide the framework for managerial policy-making. Managers must know the values of their organizations, and then they can define the behavioral implications — so that everyone understands the relevance of the value to his or her own job.

4.   Values should be actionable. A value that cannot be put into effect becomes a weakness: management should not be committed to an impossibility.

Top management should take great care not to incorporate pious hopes into their own statements of values. This means that all organizational values should be submitted to the "for instance" test. Cases should be analyzed against the espoused value to see whether it holds up in all situations. Only when senior management are convinced that they can uphold a value in all eventualities should the value be adopted.

5.   Values should enhance performance. Values are an "enabling device"; they are a means of shaping an organization to achieve its performance objectives.

Value clarification is part of the development of corporate strategy. No statement of corporate strategy is complete unless it defines the wanted values — what is needed from its people, and what is given in return. This means that there must be a logical relationship between the key success factors of an industry and the values adopted by management. For example, an airline must be seen by its potential customers as safe and helpful if it is to compete successfully; therefore, values about "doing things right" (efficiency) and "who cares wins" (fairness) are crucial.

6.   Values must be attractive and pride-giving. People should be uplifted by an organization's values. It must be possible for people to feel pride when they are playing a part in making performance objectives become a reality.

The values advocated by management must touch a deep chord within people at all levels. Values have to be respected. People feel part of a greater whole when they can identify with the organization's goals. For example, airline workers can respect their manager's concern for safety, since they have only to think of members of their own family flying on an unsafe plane to feel the importance of that value.

7. *Values should be capable of being communicated.* It is what managers do—symbolic communication—that is vital. The actions of managers must reinforce their value statements.

A key leadership task is translating values into terms that are meaningful to each individual. Managers should not adopt a value unless it is capable of being demonstrated. This means that the first group to adopt a value must themselves be managers. From time to time managers should collect data from subordinates to see what messages their unconscious behavior is communicating.

8. *Values should be written down.* Until a set of values is clear enough to be committed to paper, it will not have the authority to be a leadership statement.

The act of writing down values has three benefits: it clarifies the mind, provokes debate, and provides a message which can be communicated. It is the task of senior managers, those at the apex of the organization, to explore their own and their competitors' values and then to determine those that will provide the foundation for the organization's future. Then they must write down these values—any logical flaws will then appear!

These are the eight conditions. How are they put into effect? We have found that a sequence for value clarification is needed.

Senior managers can begin by reviewing the theory in this book and then discussing the ideas. The aim is to see whether there is a will to go further. Then a formal decision to proceed should be made. Often it is helpful to appoint a task group to check the progress of a values-clarification project and to organize the collection of data, using the questionnaire.

Often it is helpful to conduct a top team workshop to determine the core values which should prevail in the organization. Confrontation and debate are essential in order to eliminate impractical values. The members of the top team should determine what they think are the current values within the organization. The strategic plan should be reviewed to identify what values are needed to enable the organization to achieve its goals. As a final act, a Values Statement should be written.

Implementation policies should be devised which include communication strategies to cascade the message downward.[1] It is important to determine monitoring and control procedures to ensure that the program is kept on track.

Management values are detected most clearly by looking at resource decisions — a small fortune spent on decorating the director's carport and nothing spent on the workers' squalid washroom says everything — no matter what pious statements are made.

Values tend to come from the top — but not always. The values of the doctors largely create the character of a hospital. Trade unions shape some values. In Vietnam, the values of the foot soldiers, the "grunts," shaped the course of the war. Values which arise from below are sometimes productive. For example, a new top management might seek change without understanding the real competence of the other employees in the organization. Those people who are lower down in the organization often have much insight into the real values that have inspired past success. The importance of honoring history is often underestimated by a thrusting young management team. Those ethics which enabled the organization to thrive almost always have merit. The future should conserve the best of the past.

The rest of this book contains a chapter on each of the twelve values. Each chapter is an essay which is meant to provoke reaction. We do not want you always to agree with our views —

we want you to challenge them. So, if it helps, then write your comments in the margins!

Clarifying or changing organizational values will never be easy. There is much inertia built into systems. Habits run deep and therefore are resistant to change. Sustained effort is needed, especially in the beginning. This analogy helps to explain the point: a moribund organization is like a car that will not start— much effort is needed to get it moving, but once the engine starts, the car will roar away.

It will be hard to measure much effort needed to clarify personal and organizational values. By definition, there are no objective tests to measure the soundness of a value. Acts of faith are required. Debate, reflection, experiment, and conscience are essential. But, in the final analysis, the organization's value system should be a subtle consensus which binds everyone together.

Fundamental change cannot be energized from the edge of an organization. Values are decided in the "head" and the "heart" meaning that the top management cadre must be deeply involved. For this reason the chapters of this book are addressed to managers. However, those outside the key management group should not feel helpless; within their own area of authority, the values really matter to them also.

This book aims to provide a balanced and progressive management philosophy that is realistic, fair, inspiring, and positive. Establishing this philosophy will result from the implementation of each of the twelve values *at the same time*. There are checks and balances built into the theory, which help prevent tyranny or exploitation.

We hope you enjoy the process of value clarification, but don't forget that you have to do the work!

REFERENCES

1. Francis, D. (1987). *Unblocking Organizational Communication*. Aldershot, Surrey, U.K.: Gower.

PART THREE

Managing Management

C H A P T E R 4

Power: Managers Must Manage

The management group has the knowledge, authority, and position to decide the mission of the enterprise, acquire resources, and make decisions. The successful management understands the inherent power of its position and takes charge of the organization's destiny. It adopts this value: *Managers must manage.*

Management holds a unique position in any organization — it is on top. Only management people are in a position to take charge, and they must do so. Management should strive to gain and retain effective power.

There are many cases in which management has lost effective power and suffered dire consequences. On an international scale the situation in Lebanon is a chilling reminder of the chaos and inhumanity which follow the breakdown of authority.

We live in an era when the acceptance of authority is under threat. Educational, political, and cultural factors have eroded traditional values, especially over the last thirty years. For example, hospital nurses used to be treated with respect. Today they are often violently assaulted in the emergency rooms of inner-city hospitals. Crime is a way of life for many.

Organizations cannot cut themselves off from the wider society. Managers must cope with people's deep reluctance to accept discipline. Successful managements have recognized the antiauthority trends in society and have attempted to minimize their corrosive effects.

Power is gained from four sources. Each source is dependent on the others. The thesis of this book is that management should strive to capture all of the sources of power and then to retain them.

The first source of power is **ownership**. Those who have the legal title to an enterprise have rights. Managers are professional instruments, charged to act in the best interests of the owners. Legitimate authority flows down the management chain of command. This structure is relatively easy to see in the private sector; however, in the public sector, especially social services, the organization must be responsible to all of us. Sometimes public bodies create a representative group who, in effect, act as the owners; legitimate authority then flows from this source. Successful managements strengthen the owners, so that they are a potent force, and win them over, so that managers enjoy full support.

The second source of power is **information**. That which is measurable can be managed. The quality of management information systems determines how well those at the top can control and coordinate the organization. There are many cases in which effective power could not be exercised because of the ignorance of those in command. A successful management identifies the key success factors which affect its industry and ensures that the management information system speedily measures the important things.

The third source of power is **attractiveness.** A management should be able to win the hearts and minds of its employees. Attraction power comes from having a vision of the future based on sound values and then communicating this vision so that people feel that they want to be part of making it real. Communication is the true role of the leader. A successful management attracts people by what it says and what it does.

The fourth source of power is **reward and punishment**. People, unless they are perverse, do what rewards them and avoid what hurts them. Managers can control the reward/punishment system (discussed in greater length in Chapter 5). Crude carrot-and-stick methods cannot produce sustained motivation. Successful management uses rewards with subtlety.

The act of acquiring and retaining these four power sources provides the preconditions for gaining effective authority. Maintaining authority is another matter, since this requires attention, respect, and initiative.

Attention may seem a strange word to include in a discussion of power. We will explain with an example. The top management group of a German company making ladies' foundation garments in the 1950s was expert at constructing a particular type of brassiere characteristic of the era. Then there occurred the "burn the bra movement." The top management group ignored this trend and continued to construct the old-style bras. They lost market share, went bankrupt, and now are remembered only when someone turns up in an attic trunk an undergarment of the period.

The top managers of this company lost attention, failed to adapt the corporate mission to the new conditions, and lost their effective power. Henry Mintzberg, in an article on strategy,[1] points out that a successful manager, like the good craftsman, must have an intimate knowledge of the materials with which he or she is working. Management needs to pay attention to detail and to maintain the capacity to recognize important changes as they occur. The maintenance of power requires that management make sound decisions at the right time.

Respect, although a much-used word, is difficult to define. It is used when people give others the right to exert influence over them. For managers, the important insight is that respect has to be earned. This is done by competence—as discussed in the next chapter—and clarity about role. The second point requires explanation. Managers, especially those at the top, are responsible for creating the unifying identity of the organization. To accomplish this means answering the twin enduring questions — "where do we want to go?" and "how do we get there?" Only management can answer these fundamental questions. A management-defined strategic vision is necessary for organizational health. Therefore, management must

- Establish the raison d'être of the firm.
- Define the corporate mission.
- Determine what are the key success factors of the industry.
- Establish criteria and the means of performance measurement.
- Build for the future.
- Care about those whose livelihood and well-being depend on management decisions.

Failure to carry out these measures means that the organization will drift like a ship without a rudder. When this happens, those who are dependent on the wisdom of managers naturally lose respect, and management power is therefore eroded.

Initiative is closely related to attention, but is active. Management is concerned with getting things done. Power comes from taking timely action. The directors of the brassiere company lost power because they were too slow. There is an organization which suffered the opposite fate. This was a local government agency which acquired a new director who took hundreds of initiatives, such as starting studies, introducing techniques, acquiring resources, within his first six months of employment. There was much activity created, but the system became over-stressed and so morale plummeted. The director lost personal power and was replaced. His failure was poor timing. (Initiative is discussed in more depth in Chapters 7–9.) These examples show that management power depends on effective action and appropriate risk taking.

Sustaining organizational power requires constant vigilance. These guidelines, derived from careful observation, are helpful to managements that want to sustain power:

- Grant high status only to those who have repeatedly demonstrated merit.
- When an employee's performance slips for a sustained period, ensure that the person does not continue to enjoy the fruits of high status.
- Make sure that those who have high status do not get lazy.
- Avoid status symbols that block upwards communication[2]
- Do the job that you are paid to do.
- Be sure that those who report to you do the jobs that they are paid to do.

Power is easily confused with dominance, and domination is a dangerous weapon. The desire to have others submit goes deep, and such an emotion may have a biological or chemical base. A pertinent aspect of this issue is provided by the research of Professor Michael McGuire, of UCLA, who studied the brain chemistry of monkeys on the island of St. Kitts. Each colony of monkeys is led by a dominant male who threatens the other males and has the pick of the females. McGuire found that the brain of the dominant male has double the average level of the chemical serotonin in the blood stream. A dominant male isolated from the submissive gestures of his followers would lose the excess serotonin, but the new lead monkey would double his serotonin within fourteen days. Females do not experience the same chemical reaction. The alarming inference from this research is that the same reaction may occur in executives. In humans, the chemical serotonin is associated with certain kinds of mental disorders—perhaps this is the reason why the expression that absolute power corrupts contains so much truth.

The remedy to the corrupting influence of power is to adhere to the rule "do unto others as you would have them do unto you." This forces leaders to behave with the same attitudes as they seek to encourage in others.

We advocate that managers understand, acquire, and maintain power despite the inherent dangers of an authoritarian approach. We realize that locating strategic power at the top means that those lower down the organization have limits on their freedom. Despite the risks, there is no practical alternative; managers must manage.

It is a principle of military organizations that authority and responsibility go hand in hand. In practice, this is a difficult balance to maintain. Top managers tend to want to extend their authority down to the level of detail. Despite the difficulties, most successful managements place much emphasis on establishing accountabilities. They work on the principle that someone should "have the tools to do the job and be expected to perform." Being *responsible* means being "liable to be called to account both practically and ethically." Exercising authority without responsibility is dangerous because those who make the rules and enforce commands are not responsible for the outcome. Responsibility without authority is unfair; one cannot be responsible for the outcome without the ability to make decisions affecting the outcome.

Managements have been forced to move away from the crude authoritarian styles of the past; however, they are learning to cope with the issue of maintaining authority with the support of the workforce. Certainly things are not as bad as they once were. One of the authors recalls talking to a night-shift supervisor in a food factory in 1974. The man was at his wit's end because his staff simply would not work; they stayed in the cafeteria rather than performing their duties. There was a threat of physical violence. Senior management refused to back the supervisor's authority. The result was gross inefficiency and a depressed supervisor who did not know which way to turn. This situation would be much less likely to occur today. Managements have reasserted their right to manage, thereby benefiting themselves, their customers, and the communities they serve.

SUMMARY: MANAGERS MUST MANAGE — CORE BELIEFS

- Managers must exert discipline.
- The owners of the organization should be won over.
- A comprehensive management information system is essential.
- Managements need to develop their "attraction power."
- The reward/punishment system must be controlled.
- Managers must pay full attention to their tasks.
- Respect must be earned.
- Timely initiatives must be taken.
- Managers should discharge their proper role.
- High status must be earned.
- Dominance, for its own sake, should be avoided.
- Responsibility should go hand in hand with authority.

FIVE PRACTICAL STEPS TO INCREASE THE POWER OF MANAGEMENT

1. *Defining limits of authority.* Either set up a study group or get the personnel department to review the limits of authority at each level within your organization. Write the key points on a huge sheet of paper so that all gaps or overlaps are obvious. Clarify all responsibilities and check that the commensurate authorities exist. Be sure you are satisfied that the power structure in your organization is sound. Invite all your staff to comment on any changes and then redefine roles as needed.

2.   Seeking a vision of the future. Ask a random sample of people in your organization (department or larger) these two questions: What do you believe senior management's goals are? What do you respect about senior management's plans for the future? Record the comments, assess the common themes, and brainstorm practical ways to convince people in your organization to see things your way. (*Note:* this project can be formalized by using the techniques explained in *Unblocking Your Organization.*[3])

3.   Gaining authority from above. Deliberately conduct a campaign to increase the support that you receive from above. Find out what your bosses think of you (through informal conversations, reading documents, interviews, written reports, etc.) and come to an impartial assessment. Go to great lengths to convey a good impression, concentrating on overcoming any weaknesses. Use professional help to develop effective presentations.

4.   Checking the management information system. Ask all the managers and supervisors in your organization (department or larger) to write you an answer to this question: What defects in the management information system have caused your authority to be weakened over the last three months? Collect the results and invite several experts on management information systems to discuss the problems with you. Managers in large companies will have staff advisers for the purpose.

5.   Learning about your own image. Obtain at least five copies of the Power Perception Profile (Other), a validated questionnaire — from University Associates[4] and the necessary explanatory material. Ask your immediate subordinates to complete a Power Perception Profile (Other) form about you. Reflect on the results, and evaluate your personal power profile. Obtain counseling, perhaps from your personnel specialist, to assist you in understanding the results.

REFERENCES

1. Mintzberg, H. (1987, Summer), *Harvard Business Review.*
2. For a further discussion of this point, see Francis, D. (1987). *Unblocking Organizational Communication.* Aldershot, Surrey, U.K.: Gower.
3. Woodcock, M., and Francis, D. (in press). *Unblocking Your Organization.* Aldershot, Surrey, U.K.: Gower.
4. University Associates, Inc. 8517 Production Ave., San Diego, CA 92121. Telephone (619) 578-5900.

CHAPTER 5

Elitism: Cream Belongs at the Top

The management task is complex and important. The quality of people who fill management roles is crucial. An inadequate manager can wreak havoc—both by sins of commission and by sins of omission. The successful organization understands the vital importance of getting the best possible candidates into management jobs and of continuously developing their competence. It adopts this value: *Cream belongs at the top*.

"Those who enjoy power over others need to be an elite. They ought to be selected from those who are superior in intellect and character. They must be carefully trained to discharge their responsibilities with vigor and a sense of duty." This comment could have been made by a Roman general, a nineteenth-century industrialist, or a church leader. In fact, the statement was made to us by the chairman of a multinational company early in 1989.

The *Oxford Dictionary* defines an elite as "a group regarded as superior and favored." In recent years the concept of elitism has been attacked as divisive and undemocratic. Why do we advocate elitism so strongly?

In reality, some people are inherently more talented than others. The attitudes, skills, knowledge, and motivation required to achieve high competence in a specialized field is always limited. This fact should be consciously recognized by those in management who must do everything in their power to ensure that the most crucial roles in the organization are filled by a "superior" group.

In most organizations the key role is managerial, although this is not always the case. In some professional organizations, for example, the competence of a surgeon is more vital than the ability of an administrator. However, in nonprofessional organizations, the decisive resource should always be management. In Chapter 4 we argued that managers must gain and retain power. Because the responsible use of power is exceptionally demanding, it is nonsense to suggest that this should be done by those with average ability. Therefore, the successful management accepts the inevitability of elitism and seeks to mitigate its worst features by selecting, controlling, and developing elites based on genuine merit.

We have already made a comparison between the task of management and the craft system of the middle ages. A *craft* is "a calling requiring special skill and knowledge" (*Shorter Oxford Dictionary*). Medieval guilds, which were responsible for supervising the standards of their crafts members, saw that the development of true competence required seven distinct elements to be mastered. When this was done, the individual was a member of a craft elite.

The seven elements are the following:

- Practical skills which allow difficult tasks to be tackled
- Intellectual skills to solve problems
- Willingness to build for posterity
- Explicit ethical standards
- A sense of community with others engaged in the same craft

- A deep understanding of the history and development of the chosen craft
- An awareness of the contribution that the craft makes to the wider community

The costs of poor managerial craftsmanship are severe. Two examples illustrate this point. A rapidly growing food company nearly lost control of its cash flow. The company management suddenly realized that they were in crisis, despite excellent products and an unrivalled distribution system. Millions of dollars were lost, but even worse, top management did not know where the losses of cash were occurring. Only after an acutely embarrassing investigation could they pinpoint the weaknesses in financial control. The episode was properly seen by the owners as a lack of financial management craftsmanship; consequently, the senior managers were fired.

The second example is an electrical equipment manufacturer that was widely recognized as an efficient producer of household appliances. The business was declining as new technologies made the company's traditional products increasingly obsolete. Although top management discussed the problem, it did not take the bold step of investing heavily in research and development. Throughout the company, managers were told to do what they knew best: efficiently produce traditional lines. After a six-year decline, the company finally shut its doors. The blame lay with the senior managers who focused only on short-term problems; they were, in fact, poor craftsmen. We will discuss later in this chapter how to train managerial craftspeople. We believe that every person who has power over others should be a competent "managerial craftsman."

Top-quality leadership, which requires a higher set of competencies and is relatively rare, must be carefully nurtured. For example, the American army, which had discovered that few soldiers have real leadership ability, researched the reasons why only a handful of captured men escaped in the Korean War. The reason was that the communist prisoner-of-war guards carefully watched new prisoners and segregated any with leadership potential. These leaders were placed in high security confinement and watched day and night. About one in twenty soldiers received this treatment. The remainder, who were loosely guarded, lacked the leaders to mobilize escape plans. This research suggests that leadership ability is confined to about 5 percent of the population.

Management (which includes leadership skills) is vital in all kinds of organizations. This fact is illustrated by a British study made in the early 1970s. The government-funded inspectorate of schools realized that they could not properly define a "good" school. A comprehensive research program meticulously examined every aspect of ten highly regarded and successful schools. The final report came to the conclusion that the main difference between a good and a bad school was the quality of the head teacher. It is, in essence, the person at the top who determines the effectiveness of the organization.

Adopting an elitist policy costs a great deal of time and effort. The coaches of Olympic teams or commanders of elite special regiments can testify that being the best means the ruthless pursuit of superior performance. Elitism can never be a cheap option, but it is the management philosophy practiced by successful organizations.

In this chapter we define the belief and practices which enable a management elite to be developed. The important issues are selection, training, and maintenance of standards. The chapter concludes with a discussion of the risks of employing an elitist policy.

SELECTION OF ELITES

Who should fill the key roles in an organization? Attributes like intelligence, personality, track record, and skills are important. Equally important, but less often discussed, are the values held by candidates.

A management has real freedom of choice when it is recruiting or selecting. This is one occasion when the establishment holds an upper hand. We advocate this six-step approach:

1. *Define excellence:* specify what competencies can be shown that relate to superior performance.
2. *Use objective measures:* avoid applying subjective evaluation.
3. *Study the track record:* obtain a detailed and factual record of the individual's actual behavior under pressure.
4. *Explore values:* through debate and a review of past behavior, try to identify the candidate's values towards management.
5. *Test actual competence:* use extensive tests, under controlled conditions, to evaluate competence.
6. *Explore motivation:* a "hungry" candidate is more likely to perform well.

This book is not concerned with detailed techniques that have been covered elsewhere.[1] However, we wish to make this point: The majority of techniques advocated for selection are oriented towards the mass market; this, however, is not good enough. Managers can learn much from coaches of Olympic teams, commanders of crack military units, and leaders of world-famous artistic companies. They know the importance of getting the best raw material and thus go to any lengths to find extraordinary latent talent.

Some organizations have low standards of selection. We have often seen managers who spend days evaluating the potential cost/benefit of a new machine yet who employ an equally costly person after a half-hour chat. If this happens at the management level, it means double-trouble; the management job is likely to be done poorly, and subordinates likely to be stunted and frustrated.

TRAINING

Earlier in this chapter we referred to management as a craft. The training of competent managers requires that the "apprentice" is introduced to the mysteries of the managerial craft. In an earlier work we identified eleven development areas, each of which is a necessary aspect of managerial craftsmanship.[2] The key development areas are as follows:

1. **Self-management competence.** Management is a demanding task, often sapping mental and emotional energy. The craftsman manager has a deep understanding of time management and keeps fit in every sense of the word.
2. **Clear values.** Managers have to make decisions on what is worthwhile. Such choices should be based on defensible values. The craftsman manager has clear, consistent, tested values, which are felt to be right
3. **Clear goals.** The role of management is getting things done despite difficulties, which requires the capacity to focus resources on defined end results. The craftsman manager sets realistic, measurable, and challenging goals
4. **Continuous personal development.** The pace of development is so rapid that managers rapidly become obsolete if their competence does not continue to evolve. People need to take responsibility for managing their own development. The craftsman manager deliberately takes steps to grow throughout life both as a person and as a manager.
5. **Problem-solving skills.** Things going wrong is the daily grind of management. Solutions must be found to nonroutine, complex, or ambiguous issues. The craftsman manager is a skillful and methodical problem solver.

6. **High creativity.** Machines increasingly perform routine tasks, and managers have to deal with novel challenges. This requires both personal creativity and the ability to channel the talents of others. The craftsman manager is able to rise above convention, thereby finding new opportunities and solutions to difficult problems.

7. **High influence.** The capacity to persuade others is essential. It is necessary to acquire scarce resources and to win over influential people. Skills such as effective assertion, capable negotiating, and persuasive argument are relevant. The craftsman manager is an effective director of others — upwards, sideways, and below.

8. **Management insight.** Creating the right climate for people to give their best requires insightful management. This includes selecting appropriate management styles and motivating others. The craftsman manager creates an open and positive climate which gives people the support and direction that they need.

9. **High supervisory skills.** Much of management's time is spent juggling resources and reallocating priorities. Organizations must be built, systems constructed, and controls established. The craftsman manager is skillful in organizational design.

10. **Trainer capacity.** The success of a manager is measured by the efficiency of the unit which he or she controls. This means that continuous development of subordinate skills is needed, which may be done by appraisal, feedback, coaching, counselling, or direct training. The craftsman manager develops the potential of others.

11. **Team building competence.** People like to feel that they are working with others. Teamwork is important for motivational and practical reasons. Often complex activities are best coordinated through informal communication. The craftsman manager is an efficient teambuilder.

Training an elite management group requires attention to each of these eleven areas. Craft competence is developed primarily in the real world. Managers can be helped by education, training, and coaching; but they need to be put in situations where they are required to achieve important results against significant difficulties in a world in which pressures, illogicalities, and resource shortages are ever present.

The following principles of elite training have proved their worth:

- Make the training experience as real as possible.
- Ensure that the person reflects on his or her own performance.
- Give support from proven achievers.
- Devise training that develops the capacity to endure.
- Deal with all of the eleven areas that were just identified.

We are committed to developing outstanding competence in the managerial elite. It is unfortunate that many managers are less well trained than schoolteachers, plumbers, or airline pilots. Few managers have received more than rudimentary training, and, even worse, they do not take responsibility for their own development.

MAINTENANCE

Most military commanders will tell you that even the best troops lose their edge if they are not constantly being stretched. New challenges must be found, and improved techniques of development must be tried. Managers need to combine into networks in which they meet informally to discuss common concerns. It is no surprise that networks are very active in Japan and are regarded by many as the secret of business success. In the medieval guilds, networks were highly regarded by master craftsmen who found that their ideas were updated by debate and shared experience.

Management can learn from the informal operating practice of the United Kingdom parliament. Members of parliament spend some of their time together in the Palace of Westminster, in tea rooms, smoking rooms, lounges and bars, where there are almost unique networking opportunities. Much of the wisdom that has emanated from parliament over the centuries has been a direct result of the networking opportunities. In particular, the level of confrontation is sharp and merciless, which has the effect of eliminating the natural tendency to complacency in established organizations.

THE RISKS OF ELITISM

Remember the dictionary definition of an elite: it is a superior and *favored* group. Whenever a group gains privileges, there are risks that the power will be misused and that the unfavored groups will resent their subordinate position. Some interesting research by Wendy Hirsh[3] shows that a "blue-eyed boys" syndrome often develops where potential rather than performance is used for selection. Such people receive undue attention and an unfair proportion of resources. The management group becomes a self-perpetuating cadre of image-mongers rather than an elite of proven achievers. Wendy Hirsh describes the high flyer as follows: ". . . the right kind of chap. They flash around looking clever, young, quick and keen, saying all the trendy things." Such people are dangerous. Members of elites, like the master craftsmen of yesterday, need to have demonstrated their capability through performance in the real world.

Yet elites must be favored; unusual talent and dedication is rare and will disappear unless it is recognized. As we will see in the next chapter, management needs to be well rewarded in order to sustain an elite resource.

SUMMARY: CREAM BELONGS AT THE TOP — CORE PRINCIPLES

- Management should be an elite.
- Some people are naturally more talented than others.
- Elites should be chosen only on the criterion of merit.
- It is helpful to define management as a craft.
- The quality of the elite determines whether the organization will be successful.
- Adopting an elitist policy is a major managerial commitment.
- Greatest possible care should be taken when recruiting and selecting managers.
- Comprehensive training (in the eleven areas already described) is essential.
- Training techniques should be really stretching.
- The "blue eyed boys" syndrome should be avoided.
- Elites must be favored, but this should be done with caution.

FIVE PRACTICAL STEPS TO GET THE CREAM TO THE TOP OF THE MILK

1. Encourage the concept of self-development for managers. The "Unblocked Manager," as discussed before, is a technique for doing this. Obtain a copy of the book, undertake the diagnostic sections, and work through the program. If it is helpful, then take your subordinates through the same process — setting up discussion groups to act as a self-development network.
2. Get those involved in the selection of managers to spend several days shadowing the best managers in your

department. This will give them experience of real-world needs. Ask the personnel specialists to develop selection techniques which are based on performance, and then discuss their ideas in great depth.

3. Invite coaches or captains of winning sports teams to visit your organization and describe how they select and train their athletes. Arrange an informal seminar with your colleagues. Discuss how you can emulate the successful practices of the sports teams in your own organization.

4. Use teambuilding at the top of your organization to develop an elite. The methods and questionnaires in "Team Development Manual"[4] and "Improving Work Groups"[5] help to accomplish this.

5. Invite everyone responsible for management training in your organization to write a one thousand word paper entitled "Good management is. . . ." Ask the members of your team to evaluate the results against their own views and principles. Enter into a detailed debate with the trainers so that they are fully aware of your needs and wants.

REFERENCES

1. See Jones, J. and Woodcock, M. (1986). *Manual of Management Development*. Aldershot, Surrey, U.K.: Gower.
2. See Woodcock, M., and Francis, D. (1982). *The Unblocked Manager*. Aldershot, Surrey, U.K.: Gower.
3. *Institute of Manpower Studies Review* (1985, June). University of Sussex, Brighton, U.K.
4. Woodcock, M. (1989). *Team Development Manual*. 2d ed. Aldershot, Surrey, U.K.: Gower.
5. Francis, D. and Young, D. (1979). *Improving Work Groups*. San Diego, CA: University Associates.

CHAPTER 6

Reward: Performance Is King

The performance of those who lead an organization is crucial. Managers need to perform consistently and energetically in pursuit of the organization's goals. The successful organization identifies and rewards success. It adopts this value: *Performance is king*.

As consultants on organizational effectiveness, we are often asked to help companies that have lost their way and are struggling to survive. It is a difficult task. Invariably there are many problems — poor systems, untrained staff, inadequate investment, low morale, weak marketing, high costs, and so on.

One such organization, referred to here as The Metal Skills Company, occupied a run-down site in the back streets of a traditional manufacturing town. For years the company had been near bankruptcy. Having been asked by Bob Greenway, the Chief Executive, to advise on improvements, we undertook a thorough study. Almost every possible organizational ailment existed in the company. The sickness was apparent to all; but the solutions remained obscure.

Fortunately, The Metal Skills Company made a range of products that were marketable. The major problem was that the manufacturing procedures were wasteful, ponderous, costly, un-controlled, and overmanned. We advised that all management efforts be directed towards a radical overhaul of the manufactur-ing system. This meant introducing "Just in Time" manufacturing for low-cost flexibility, "Total Product Quality" for improved stan-dards, and "Quality Circles" for increased employee involvement.

Such changes would require a revolution in attitudes, skills, behavior, and organization. Bob Greenway became convinced intellectually of the need for change, but not emotionally. We suggested that he visit a number of factories in Japan and Korea. He returned shaken but nonetheless resolute. From then on the change program received his wholehearted support, because he had seen the strength of the competition. Greenway addressed a staff meeting as follows: "We have no option. We must compete or die. I am to blame for waking up too slowly to the challenge that we face. But I have learned my lesson. From today, every action that we take must be questioned. We must review all our habits, and discard those which do not add value to our products. One principle must underlie everything that we do — it is results that count. Everything else is irrelevant. There are no legitimate excuses."

The effects of Bob Greenway's speech were disappointing. Some employees felt that the speech was a scare tactic, while others were confused by the new concepts. Nothing changed. Greenway decided on a bold investment; he sent a group of ten managers, supervisors, and trade-union representatives to retrace his steps around the manufacturing plants of Japan and Korea. He chose the group carefully, selecting those whose opinions guided others.

The effect was electrifying. The group returned determined to transform The Metal Skills Company into a "world class manufacturing unit." The company made another major invest-ment, purchasing a six-hour set of videos on new manufacturing philosophies. Everyone in the manufacturing division, from sweeper to general manager, saw these videos twice. They learned that Japanese managers in the Toyota company had perfected

"Just in Time" techniques in the 1960s and 1970s. Industry in the USA had discovered the benefits in 1980 when General Electric, Kawasaki, and Toyota trucks, in Long Beach, California, began to use the concepts.

The Metal Skills Company's management felt that they had to go the same route. They had attempted participative management a decade earlier, but the benefits had been transient. The problem is familiar. As Robert Reich[1] put it: "Management consultants espoused 'Theory Y' or, better still, 'Theory Z.' But these factory-tested techniques for making workers feel better simply created a facade of workplace collaboration. The distinction between thinkers and doers remained intact." This time the company managers decided to commit themselves to a total revolution. Task groups were established to install "Just in Time" manufacture, "Total Product Quality," and "Quality Circles." They also did much research. The company was no longer ignorant of the techniques needed.

Within two years The Metal Skills Company was exporting to Japan, and its renaissance was featured in the national press. The company had ruthlessly eliminated wasteful systems and behavior, and took pride in its international competitiveness. How had it been achieved? The Metal Skills Company had adopted the value: *Performance is king.*

The value "performance is king" was incorporated in the company's culture, meaning that the reward system had to be changed. In this chapter we will examine rewards that shape the values of the total organization.

Benefits, which are controlled from the top of the organization, are the manager's tool kit for shaping behavior at work. Reward and punishment are primary techniques for influencing and controlling others. The ability to reward and punish is a source of power. The saying "he who pays the piper calls the tune" is true—at least in part. The successful management uses reward and punishment systems for aligning the organization toward sustaining high performance.

It has taken a long time for managers to recognize the creative power of the reward system. For example, Rank Xerox made the newspapers[2] in 1988 when it announced that the merit payments for its senior managers would partly depend on customers' feedback. An annual survey was to be conducted: if customers thought ill of the firm, then the poor feedback reduced the pay of the responsible managers. It is surprising that such measures were not put in place years earlier.

Reward and punishment affects (conditions) the ways we behave. People, like other animals, seek satisfaction while avoiding pain. How should people be rewarded so that they will adopt the value: *performance is king?*

Reward power can be used in five key ways; consider these illustrations:

1. **Attracting able people**: "We need a brilliant chemist. Search the world. Make an offer that can't be refused."
2. **Demonstrating relative value**: "Top-quality salespeople are vital. We will pay them as much as the Chief Executive."
3. **Showing that merit wins the day**: "Jones has succeeded where Smith did not. We will promote Jones."
4. **Shaping behavior**: "From January 1st, salesmen will have an increased proportion of their earnings related to the degree of satisfaction of their customers."
5. **Integrating effort**: "Every department is expected to present its plans for improving interdepartmental communication within one month."

Reward systems actually influence the thinking process. This process was well described by one manager: "In our company managers are paid a 10 percent bonus on profitability against targets. If we don't meet target — then we don't get the bonus: it's as simple as that. We also get a 1 percent additional bonus for each percentage point of profit over 10 percent — up to a maximum of bonus 20 percent in total. This year began well, and senior management relaxed, spending a lot of time in long-term planning. Then our margins came under threat, and it's now hell for leather to make budget. No one talks about the bonus, but, like the threat of imminent hanging, it certainly concentrates the mind."

Reward systems should be devised to reinforce high performance. The example in the preceding paragraph illustrates the point. Current theories of motivation provide useful guidelines. "Expectancy theory" is now widely accepted, and the lessons are of real practical value. The key points are as follows:

- Attitudes, beliefs, values, and perceptions should be studied in great detail. Well-constructed attitude surveys are a useful tool with which to gain this information.
- Rewards are best oriented toward individual performance, not given as "across the board" rises.
- People should know exactly how rewards are allocated so that it is quite obvious that high performance brings high reward; making this known requires an effective communication program.
- Training should emphasize that high rewards can be realized through high performance.
- Everyone's goals should be clearly identified, and managers should strive to remove blockages to goal attainment.
- Those who support nonproductive values should be encouraged to realize that these do not lead to personal success.

Adopting these six guidelines is a practical way of saying that "performance is king." The first battle is to win the hearts and minds of the management cadre. In turn, managers shape the attitudes and values of all other employees. Senior managers should use the reward system to align thinking, by using rewards to create a definition of organizational "reality" that molds people's values and standards into a consistent pattern, acting like a magnet on iron filings.

Rewards are sometimes given for no objective performance achievement. Then people's behavior goes haywire, and management lacks the tools to reestablish standards. An oblique illustration comes from the People's Republic of China, where the government conducted a study on the problem of the notoriously rude shop assistants of Peking. The 1984 report found that it was commonplace to see customers pleading with idle shop workers for service, even weeping to get a response. Rudeness, incivility, and even physical violence were observed. The government report explained that shop staffs had total security of employment, with their bonuses and wages guaranteed, and so they lacked any incentive to perform to an acceptable level. After the report was published, action was taken. Shop staffs are now being measured by performance, like other parts of the Chinese economy. On a recent visit, the author, observing the major effects these changes are having on the general well-being, commented that it is, in part, the reward system adopted by the Chinese Government that is bringing about radical change and newfound prosperity.

The "performance is king" value has two implications; the first is that everyone must have an accurate personal definition of excellent performance, and the second is that nonperformance-related activities must be pruned back.

The technique of management by objectives (MBO) emphasizes that everyone should know what outputs are required from their work but should be allowed to choose the means of accomplishment. This is the essential ingredient in performance management. The MBO ritual—annual cycle, full documentation, and formalized procedures—is often unhelpful, but the intention is right. As users of the techniques in the best-selling *One Minute Manager*[3] will realize, the basic tenets of management by objectives are invaluable.

Much organizational resource is wasted on tangential activities. This tendency has to be ruthlessly watched. Energy diverted into things which are "nice," not essential, can erode the obsessive commitment characteristic of successful organizations. Performance, for its own sake, is the driving force. The successful manager inculcates a principle that results are the first criterion of success with the dedication of a mountain climber who risks his life to reach the top of a difficult peak: because it is there.

Despite all their good intentions, managers often find it difficult to implement the "performance is king" principle. How do you measure the contribution of the public relations manager or the head teacher in a school? It is difficult, but not impossible, to quantify. In such cases worth can be assessed only by comparing the person's performance against a standard. In our consulting practice, we have found that six reward strategies are a useful practical guide. These are as follows:

1. Be explicit about what constitutes success in each job.
2. Reward positive behavior with above-average material benefits.
3. Reward positive behavior with above-average recognition.
4. Use all possible persuasion techniques (leadership, media, communication, etc.) to orientate group norms to high performance.
5. Create opportunities for people to feel good about using their skills and knowledge.
6. Deal with low standards of performance.

There are many difficulties in implementing these six reward strategies. It is easier in the management group because they are disposed to be supportive. Successful organizations find ways of taking the "performance is king" ethic down to the lowest level.

However, there is a common barrier which applies to some management groups and many other parts of the work force. Both managers and trade unionists realized long ago that reward and punishment systems are crucial devices for achieving compliance. Historically, trade unions have sought to reduce managers' power by standardizing payment structures on a nonperformance basis. Since a "good" employee performs much better than a "bad" employee, it must be a principle of successful managements that they, not trade unions, control the policies of the organizational reward/punishment system.

All the managers that we have asked believe in inequality. They are troubled because it is difficult to recognize and reward the real differences between people. For example, many crafts-men who have given thirty years of excellent service have inferior status and privileges to their seventeen-year-old typist daughters who are classed as white-collar staff. The principle is clear: managers need to do everything that they can to recognize and reward high performance.

Reward/punishment systems meet this requirement if they are

- Based on a fair and equitable method of measuring performance
- Easy to understand
- Straightforward to monitor
- Flexible to meet unpredicted needs
- Supported by the representatives of relevant interest groups
- Linked to career and performance improvement

Financial reward is an imperfect motivator. It has been wisely said that "the promise of a good salary will get someone to work each day, but it won't encourage hard work." The psychological rewards—like challenge, recognition, fear of failure, and personal power—must be employed. Above all, there is one basic motivator: belonging. People are, at root, tribal animals. Mankind's sophistication is relatively recent. Insightful managers take advantage of a person's basic need to belong by making the person feel valued only when he or she is performing to a high standard. Managers have to realize that they are the emotional leaders of their departments and organizations.

Low levels of performance can usually be observed when psychological rewards are neglected. Successful managements use rewards to energize people and get them working for the organization. They train all their managers to implement the subtle motivational techniques which give challenge, provide recognition, set demanding targets, and enable people to feel genuinely important contributors.

This chapter concludes with some cautionary words. The relentless drive for performance can become demonic, to quote the term used by Roger Harrison, an experienced analyst of management cultures.[4] By this, Harrison means that moral standards are discarded in a ruthless search for output and profit. Performance should be king, but not God.

SUMMARY: CORE PRINCIPLES — PERFORMANCE IS KING

- Reward and punishment are primary techniques for influencing and controlling others.
- Rewards should be used to align people to work for management's goals.
- Managers' rewards must be orientated towards performance.
- The expectancy theory of motivation should be carefully studied by managers.
- Everyone should understand the reward system.
- People should focus their attention on results — not on diversions.
- Positive behavior should always be rewarded.
- Negative behavior cannot be allowed to go unchallenged.
- Every system or convention which undermines fair reward for performance must be fought.
- Managers need to be expert in nonfinancial rewards.

- A performance culture must not be allowed to become "demonic."

FIVE PRACTICAL STEPS FOR REWARDING PERFORMANCE

1. Invite a management psychologist from a business school to arrange for your team a half-day seminar on the topic of "Reward and Punishment in Management." Tell the psychologist that you want to hear a summary of the latest research, including the work of Professor Lawler.[5] Discuss the effectiveness of your current approach to rewarding high performance and confronting low performance. Conclude with a checklist of action steps.

2. Explore ways of training your managers to be more skillful in techniques of giving psychological rewards. Techniques such as providing job enrichment,[6] positive feedback,[7] transactional analysis,[8] and coaching,[9] are useful. Ask your training department to prepare a course, ensuring that plenty of skill practice is built in. Attend the pilot course, in full, before you commit your managers to attending.

3. Study the policies on rewards that any staff associations or trade unions have. Get to know the officials of these organizations to see how they think. Determine whether there is any means of strengthening the payment for performance principle in practice.

4. Keep alert to the need to change your incentive system every few years. There is much evidence that such systems lose their effectiveness over time. Adopt a policy of continuous experimentation to see what new techniques for increasing incentive might be of value.

5. Collect data from the managers, and any other relevant groups, about what motivates and demotivates them.

Use a validated questionnaire for the purpose.* Your personnel manager or a competent consultant will be able to help. Arrange for the results of the survey to be presented to a meeting of your team, and decide on practical steps to improve motivation. Set targets and regularly monitor the effectiveness of your program.

REFERENCES

1. Reich, R. (1983). *The New American Frontier*. New York: Times Books.
2. Financial Times, London, p. 13, 2/17/88.
3. Blanchard, K., and Johnson, S. (1988). *The One Minute Manager*. New York: William Morrow.
4. Harrison, R. (1983, Fall). Strategies for a New Age. *Human Resource Management*, 22, 3, 209–235.
5. Lawler, E. (1971). *Pay and Organizational Effectiveness: A Psychological View*. New York: McGraw-Hill.
6. Hertzberg, F. (1968). *Work and the Nature of Man*. New York: Staples Press.
7. Blanchard, K. and Johnson, S. (1988). *The One Minute Manager*. New York: William Morrow.
8. Berne, E. (1968). *Games People Play*. New York: Ballantine.
9. Hague, H. (1973). *Management Development for Real*. London: Institute of Personnel Management.

---

* The *Management of Motives Index* and *Work Motivation Inventory* are two suitable instruments. They are available from University Associates, Inc., 8517 Production Ave., San Diego, CA 92121.

PART FOUR

Managing the Task

CHAPTER 7

Effectiveness: Doing the Right Thing

Focusing on the right issues must be a constant concern. Unless effort is well directed, somewhere a smarter management will find ways of taking your market. A successful organization is able to focus resources on activities that get results. It adopts this value: *Do the right thing.*

In the back streets of a prosperous city a scientific instruments manufacturer locked its doors for the last time. Founded in the 1920s by an entrepreneurial scientist who had pioneered a new technique for analyzing trace chemical elements, the company became a watchword for manufacturing reliable and innovative products. For many years it had been a world-famous company; about ten years ago, the prosperous company was purchased from its elderly owner by a multinational conglomerate on a buying spree. New management was installed under a so-called professional chief executive — a distinguished accountant a few years from retirement.

Under the new chief executive's stewardship, things did not go well. Investment was pruned with savage contempt for anything but immediate advantage, and new products were not developed; consequently, corporate vitality evaporated. Competitors, who saw the weakness in their most respected rival, seized the market. Orders slowed to a trickle. The chief executive cut investment even further as he strove to balance the books. Older employees witnessed the destruction of their once proud company and boldly stated that the new management policy was wrong. They were ignored. Those with marketable skills left for new jobs, while the longest-serving employees labored on with foreboding.

Then one day two chauffeur-driven limousines visited the factory; the men from corporate head office had arrived. After they had spent half the day touring the plant and inspecting the doleful accounts, they decided to close the company. The story has a sad ending. The craftsmen, instrument makers, assemblers, and clerical workers who had spent their lives contributing their excellent skills were thrown out of work with nothing more than a standard word-processed letter of regret from a distant executive.

What was the cause of the decline and fall of the scientific instrument company? Simple. The new chief executive did the wrong thing—and did it repeatedly.

There are many reasons for decline. Stuart Slatter,[1] who has made a study of companies that have gone into near-terminal decline, concludes that the most powerful poison is a domineering chief executive who fails to listen.

The other causes of the failure of commercial companies are as follows:

An ineffective top team: either weak individuals, functionally specific contributions, poor communication, and/or a lack of consensus

Neglect of the core business: frittering away energy on divergent issues.

Lack of management depth: having inexperienced, undereducated or low-achieving individuals in key positions

Complacent belief in evolution: not seeing the need for radical change

All of these factors can create a situation in which managers do the wrong thing. We assert in Chapter 4 that power must be grasped by management, meaning that key decisions should always be made by the senior management group. There can be no valid excuses if the organization is misdirected. Only the management can be blamed either for indecision or for the wrong decision.

No one can guarantee right decision making at the top. A decision is a combination of analysis, hunch, hope, and belief; and decision making is a fallible process, limited by the knowledge and talent of those with power. However, not all is lost. Much can and should be done to improve the knowledge of decision makers, enhance the talents of the top team, and improve the process by which all the necessary ingredients come together.

As we emphasized in chapter 5, it is vital to ensure that the apex of the organization is staffed with able people. It is one of the ironies of management life that, despite the millions of unemployed people, talented and available senior executives are as rare as bank notes lying in the street. Even when able individuals are recruited, the story has just begun.

Pioneering work by Meredith Belbin,[2] discussed further in Chapter 10, demonstrated that senior management teams that are capable of doing things right are built from diverse individuals. His analysis strongly indicates that the kernel of wise decision making is a balanced top team that includes creative thinkers, critics, conceptualizers, and results-oriented individuals. There are several interesting implications of the analysis. First, top teams should avoid the trap of looking for a group composed of similar people — a wide spread of competence is the key. Second, power struggles often occur when strong individuals (called *shapers*) are in the same team — hence the need for judicious selection to prevent excessive personal conflict. Last, team building is essential — members have to perceive each other's strengths and learn to respect differences.

The possession of the right ingredients alone does not make a good cake! The members of a top team need to understand that their role is quite distinct from middle management. They are the guardians of mission and strategy. Fundamental decisions about values, resources, priorities, tactics, and aims can be made only at the top. The senior management need to have a shared understanding of the legacy that they wish to leave behind them. (This is especially true for noncommercial organizations.) Such strategic decision making requires specialized expertise — just as a steeplejack requires different skills from those of a bricklayer.

Should you make the assumption that all that is required is for the organization to have an able, balanced, and skilled top team? The answer is no! An effective management process has to be in place. Managers can learn much about effective decision-making processes by studying the ways in which the world's most important issues are resolved in government. In the U.S. Senate, there are a number of conventions that serve to improve the quality of decision making. These are as follows:

1. Key issues are exhaustively debated by people with varied points of view.
2. No one allows politeness to prevent vigorous probing and questioning.
3. Opposition is deliberately encouraged.
4. People with special interests are invited to present their points of view.
5. There is a huge machine designed to provide valid information for the decision makers.
6. Those who make decisions are forcefully reminded of the outcomes of their choices.
7. Lying is seen as unacceptable.

The important insight gained from studying the parliamentary model is that decision making should never be allowed to happen in a closed system; those at the top should constantly be challenged, made to be truthful, and held accountable. When this happens, there is a greater possibility that the right things will be done. Doing the right things is more likely when open government prevails. By exposing issues honestly, using the guidelines that parliament has evolved over the centuries, the chances of wise decision making are increased.

For commercial companies, this observation means having a strategy for sustaining a competitive edge. From Michael Porter[3] we learn that there are only three distinct competitive strategies: being the cheapest (cost leadership), being special (differentiation), or spotlighting a narrow area for concentration (focus). It is vitally important that top managers understand which competitive strategy they should use and then ruthlessly pursue their chosen direction.

For example, General Motors, in most of the countries in which it operates, seeks to be the overall cost leader. It aggressively seeks market share so that it can enjoy economies of scale, vigorously pursues cost reduction, keeps a stranglehold on overhead, avoids low-volume markets, and studies the costs of competitors. Another company, Porsche, chooses to differentiate, with the aim of being perceived by the customer as providing a significantly better product. This means investing in being perceived as being unique, finding valued differences, and being either fashionable or novel. The strategies of both companies are very different; and, in order to do the right thing, everyone in both companies needs to know exactly what is important. One of the authors has visited production plants of both companies and talked to senior management in both. They are both successful — in that they do the right thing, but in different ways.

Noncommercial organizations have a more complex task in establishing their mission: one organization may see its purpose as contributing to sustaining current patterns of life (like the police force), or another may define its role as helping to build a better future (as a theater might aim to do). Since there is no standardized way to measure "contribution to the social good," strategic decision makers in such organizations are advised to use something like the parliamentary process described before in order to improve the quality of their top management process and to find a viable mission.

Many senior managers are aware of their decision-making responsibilities. The chairman of a large public company told us, "Above all I must be positive and realistic. Excessive optimism will place the company in jeopardy. Pessimism, on the other hand, stunts initiative and stultifies creative minds. Realism is more difficult; if I make wrong judgments, then I lead people astray. My task is to do everything possible to see that the right judgments are made at the right time."

Once the mission is clear, the task has then just begun. Doing the right thing requires a commitment to evaluate factual data and confront reality. Managers should be practical scientists who do not fall into the trap of defining subjective perception as truth. They need to define systems which collect and organize strategic data. As any army commander will tell you, this is at the heart of effective decision making.

A colleague, Bob Garratt,[4] says that the subconscious ways in which managers organize their thought processes (psychologists call the patterns *constructs*) are vitally important. This observation makes sense. A manager who sees the organizational world in terms of entries on a balance sheet is unlikely to perceive or respect qualitative data. Garratt describes four basic constructs which senior managers use to guide themselves. Each has its limitations, and managers who fail to use all four are likely to do the wrong thing—especially those who, in Garratt's words, are "bound by the conceptual shackles of traditional specialization."

By adapting Garratt's observation, we can define four models:

1.   *The functionalist view:* Top managers see their world in terms of the classic functions like production, sales, and finance. They pay some attention to the environment and their markets, but only through the existing organizational structure. Typically, such organizations have little teamwork at the top; there is little to discuss because most tasks are broken down into functional responsibilities.

2. *The functionally responsive view:* Top managers continue to see the world in functional terms but develop their teamwork so that they deal with a wider range of issues — like social and economic changes and issues of ethics. Managers still see themselves as heads of functions, but the quality of debate is much improved.

3. *The power groupings view:* Top managers see their task in terms of dealing with those who have power over the organization. This includes the owners, the public, the consumers, and those who provide labor or inputs into the system. When top managers take this viewpoint, they are less likely to be trapped into interpreting everything through functional blinders.

4. *The competitive quality view:* Top managers define what their organization does that gives value to the world. They think about four aspects: the quality of business performance, the quality of consumer service, the quality of working life, and the quality of social responsibility. This way of thinking focuses attention on contribution and requires careful identification of the ingredients of competitiveness. It leads to defining the organization's task in terms of worth. Thus, a commercial company that thinks in this way will be concerned with the reasons why customers should be satisfied, and sees profitability as a measure of success.

There is no single "right" way to think about management. Flexibility in the use of constructs is the key to success. Able managers look at their world in a number of different ways, conducting a series of intellectual experiments and building up a comprehensive picture from many fragmented insights.

The Japanese, who are no strangers to organizational success, adopt a particularly focused approach to improving the quality of decision making. They emphasize the importance of allowing time for thought — using the techniques of meditation and consensus. They realize that some decisions are vastly more important than others and that it pays to invest a great deal of thought to get the basics right.

For the western observer, the process seems to move with almost painful slowness. Options are discussed time and time again. Time is allocated to meditate on the issues and see what the intelligence of the unconscious mind says on the issue. Consensus is sought even when the majority shares a common view. Finally, when a decision is made, the process has brought two advantages: depth and commitment. The ground rules ensure that issues are examined in depth, so that the chances of superficial analysis are minimal. In addition, everyone concerned has played a part in the decision and understands the commitments needed. The entire management team moves with speed and clarity; it is like the story of the tortoise and the hare, only played on a huge scale.

There is one final idea that we must describe. It is wrong to imagine that a well-constructed and able team with efficient psychological and operational processes will always succeed. In its competence there lurks a destructive worm. It was a political scientist, Professor Janus,[5] who opened our eyes to a great enemy of right decision making, which he called "groupthink." When important decisions have to be made, often it is natural for a small group of powerful people to determine what should be done. This avoids the convoluted complexity of democratic systems and the obvious risk of tyranny in a despotic regime. However, Janus found that the members of close groups begin to think alike, look only to others within the group for support, and ignore all evidence that suggests that their views are wrong. Such groups unconsciously establish "mind guards" that prevent disturbing facts from being heard, and they feel themselves to be superior in wisdom. Their decision making becomes suspect, and travesties of judgment are commonplace. Ironically, the closeness of the decision-making team contributes to the decline in their capacity as effective decision makers.

These are the managerial ingredients which increase the chances that management will do the right thing. In the last analysis, there is no remedy for incompetence in positions of power. Nevertheless, much can be done to reduce risks and confront problems as they occur. For the sake of all those who work in the organization and who are affected by it, it is vital to work constantly to do the right thing.

SUMMARY: CORE PRINCIPLES – DOING THE RIGHT THING

- Domination is dangerous.
- Management cannot escape its responsibility for decision making.
- Every care should be taken to ensure that there is an able and balanced top team.
- Top managers need to understand every aspect of their role.
- Senior managers need to have a shared understanding of the legacy that they wish to leave.
- An effective management information system is the basis of good decision making.
- Managers can learn much from reviewing how political decision-making systems work.
- No organization should be a closed system.
- Commercial organizations need to be completely clear about their competitive strategy.
- It pays to look at the management task from a number of different perspectives.
- Meditation and consensus seeking are valuable tools in the predecision phase.
- "Groupthink" should be understood and avoided.

FIVE PRACTICAL STEPS TO ENCOURAGE DOING THE RIGHT THING

1. Take steps to develop the decision-making skills of senior managers. Get several business schools to put together a presentation after looking at your needs. Invite their consultants to sit in on your senior team meetings to get firsthand understanding of your strengths and weaknesses.

2. Identify your three best competitors and collect information about their decision-making mechanisms. Perhaps set up a project group to conduct a detailed comparison between you and the opposition. On a historical graph showing their performance, plot the key decisions that they have made. Study how they approached the decision-making task and try to learn the lessons.

3. Obtain a copy of "The Groupthink Audit"[6] and get senior teams to complete it. This will help assess from a psychological viewpoint the strengths and weaknesses of the top team's decision making. Perhaps an experienced team facilitator would be helpful. The Audit contains practical suggestions about techniques for reducing the risk of groupthink.

4. Experiment with using the services of a "nonexecutive director" to contribute to decision making at senior levels. Invite an experienced manager to act as a catalyst in decision-making meetings. Try a number of different individuals, to study the effect of different personalities and skills.

5. Set up a video camera at several senior team meetings and get an editor to produce a half-hour film which typifies the process of the meeting. Show the video immediately prior to the next meeting, and then have the group brainstorm ways of improving the team's process.

REFERENCES

1. Slatter, S. (1988). *Corporate Recovery*. Harmondsworth, U.K.: Penguin Books.
2. Belbin, M. (1981). *Management Teams — Why They Succeed and Fail*. New York: Halsted Press.
3. Porter, M. E. (1980). *Competitive Strategy*. New York: Free Press.
4. Garratt, R. (1987). *The Learning Organization*. London: Fontana.
5. Janus, I. L. (1972). *Victims of Groupthink*. Boston: Houghton Mifflin.
6. In Francis, D. (1987). *50 Activities for Unblocking Organizational Communication*. Aldershot, U.K.: Gower.

Efficiency: Doing Things Right

It has been said that good management is about doing hundreds of little things well. All too often a small error has a disproportionate effect on the quality of the whole. The drive to do everything well gives a sharp edge. The successful organization relentlessly searches for better ways to do things, and it constantly builds pride into the job. It adopts this value: *Do things right*.

The authors began writing this chapter on a flight from London to New Zealand. The journey had started badly. After encountering delays on the way to the airport, we arrived just in time for the flight. As we struggled onto the plane, with a portable computer, suitbags, etc., the cabin crew watched us with laconic disinterest. We had been looking forward to the luxury of faultless first-class airline service, imagining that our journey would be like a TV advertisement. Needless to say, the opposite was the case. We were shown to our seats by a flight attendant who used the "correct" phrases taught to her in airline school, but her manner was jaded and her concern was plastic. We began to get settled for the twenty-five hour flight. When one of our bags would not fit into the front wardrobe, the flight attendant ordered us to take it to the larger closet by the exit, and then she vanished. During the journey, every request to the cabin staff met with a grudging acquiescence. We noticed dozens of minor incidents, innuendoes, oversights, and overall slipshod service. We both felt like passengers on a commuter bus journey, not first class international jet-setters. From one point of view, the blemishes were minor, and it would have seemed petty to complain. However, our memory of the flight is sour, so that it is doubtful whether we will willingly fly this airline again. In many ways the flight staff "did the wrong thing."

Somewhere over the Atlantic we began to think about this situation from a management point of view. What would we do if we were senior executives of that airline? No doubt those executives had debated what image they wanted to present and had then enshrined their customer service standards in a well-phrased charter. The reality, though, was different. The crew went through the motions, but they did not care. In trying to understand the causes of the mediocre service, we found ourselves analyzing categories of organizations in which there was a demonstrated concern to do things right.

Our first line of inquiry was historic: "Why was it that Great Britain, a small island with few obvious advantages, should have become the birthplace of the Industrial Revolution and become, for many years, the world's most successful economy?"

The answer to this question is found, in part, in an analysis of social values. From the early eighteenth century, a new spirit of invention, entrepreneurship, and dedication began to thrive. It became commonplace for machines to do the work of people. Efficient (for the times) factories replaced independent craftsmen. Increasingly, wealth was created by industrial enterprise, rather than by agriculture. By the time that Queen Victoria came to the throne, Britain was the "workshop of the world." It is illuminating to examine the factors which led to such a successful combination of attitudes and behavior. (After all, most managers, including airline executives, are trying to stimulate a similar process in their own organizations today.)

Perhaps the best explanation of the causes of the British Industrial Revolution was, ironically, presented by a German. Max Weber, whose book *The Protestant Ethic and the Spirit of Capitalism*[1] provided a profound analysis. The title says it all. Weber argued that Protestant beliefs convinced people that they should fulfill themselves through achievement and hard work in this world, rather than devoting themselves to contemplating the life hereafter. Eighteenth-century Britain, almost alone in the world, was a society without a fatalistic acceptance of the status quo. The motto "if a job is worth doing, it is worth doing well" became current. Hard work was seen as virtuous, and the embryonic middle class epitomized the diligent values of the times.

Many of the inspired founders of the Industrial Revolution shared the ethics of the nineteenth-century American pioneers — they believed that personal values were important and that everyday life had a meaning above mere self-interest. People were taught to believe that one's merit in this life was dependent on the amount of care and attention that was invested in daily tasks.

This simple belief gave direction to the greatest changes in economic productive capacity in the history of humankind. The principles advocated were that people are responsible for their fortune in life, and their fortune depends on diligence and attention to detail. The same theme occurred in all walks of life. Baden-Powell's often-repeated advice to the Boy Scout movement (of which he was the founder) that "stickability" is a primary virtue led to generations of young people striving to see things through.

Times change; the Protestant ethic is no longer an inspiration to many people. If the history books are to be believed, many nineteenth-century workers possessed the attitudes that most managers would like to see displayed today. Today's managers face a dilemma; they need people to adopt diligent attitudes, yet they cannot rely on accepted social values to inculcate them.

Behavior is based on well-articulated and frequently repeated beliefs that are held as precious by those who shape opinions in the community. If the values of the wider society do not support efficiency and effectiveness, then managers have no option; they must fight against the current social trends and inculcate the "right" values. They have to win the battle for the hearts of the work force.

Successful organizations are capable of doing this. They have learned the basic truth that "doing things right" is an essential ethic. The modern form of this enduring insight is the quality improvement programs that companies like IBM, Scandinavian Airways, and Woolworth have undertaken. A managing director conveyed the principle exactly when he commented to us that "Persistence is everything. When people set inner standards, their performance is improved from within. This means that people take greater responsibility for their working lives. This is the ethos that I try to create. But it's a hard battle. Society has largely lost the standards of hard work. Many people want something for nothing. We have to swim against the tide, but when this is done, the individual feels a great satisfaction — pride of accomplishment."

It is possible to develop an organizational culture that promotes "doing things right." Successful concerns as diverse as hamburger stores, opera houses, and prisons have shown that it is possible to devise and sustain a high-performing organizational culture.

The recent history of Jaguar cars is a case in point. "Doing things right" was an obsession of Sir William Lyons, the founder of the Jaguar company. Unfortunately, his ethic was lost when this once-proud sports car manufacturer was swallowed up by a gargantuan bureaucracy in a fit of government-inspired "rationalization." In the late 1970s Jaguar was nearly bankrupt. Although the company had a fine basic product, a skillful — but inefficient — work force, and a potentially viable niche in the market, the product quality was appalling. When John Egan became managing director in 1980, he was determined to remedy the carelessness which had plagued every aspect of production. The whole company had to rediscover the merits of doing things right. This process began with suppliers, and touched every aspect of production, marketing, sales, and customer care. The program of organizational relearning was achieved through management development, intensive communication, pruning of deadwood, worker involvement, and the development of efficient control systems. A tireless pursuit of perfection was the only solution to Jaguar's problems.

Organizations do not have any choice but to work on developing a diligent culture. Competition from countries in the Pacific Basin is razor sharp. A colleague who had returned from a month's study tour of Japan remarked, "They don't have any secrets, it's just that they follow through on everything. Western companies must rediscover the spirit of quality."

How is this done? Senior managers must be fully committed to the principle of doing things right. Then the message must be cascaded down the organization. The processes needed are persuasion and indoctrination. Both words smack of "brainwashing" and, if the truth be told, managers do need to acquire some of the skills of the propagandist. There are five issues that need to be addressed:

- Managers need to be completely clear about their core performance standards.
- Only a few (not more than four) performance themes can be followed at any one time.
- Each manager, supervisor, and worker should know exactly what the standards mean in relation to his or her actual tasks.
- Each individual worker should feel that he or she is being fairly treated, so that the worker will buy into company standards.
- An energetic and comprehensive program of persuasive communication should be constantly pursued.[2]

It is important that managers realize that they communicate standards by symbolic actions — the actual behavior of leaders sets the tone. No organization will do things right unless those who have power practice what they preach. Managers need to instruct people to do everything well, even to the smallest details, such as how to water the office plants. Every time that casual standards are accepted, the principle of doing things right is underminded. This means that managers must become very selective about what they actually do. Since sloppy performance cannot be tolerated, it is important to be precise about what the organization is dedicated to achieve.

The power of the concept is demonstrated by the sustained success of the Mars company. It has been an ethic of the company, long practiced by the founder, Forest Mars, that everyone works—and is seen to work. All employees, from the managing director to junior typist, are required to clock in and out. Laziness is almost unthinkable. A Mars manager told us, "We are action orientated, but everyone makes damn sure that they do things really well. This is not a company that accepts a casual approach."

As part of our research into the impact of values on company culture, one of the authors undertook a comparative study of two factories making identical products—one factory was in England and the other in the United States. Each had similar equipment, used the same ingredients, had comparable overhead costs, and made the same brands of convenience foods. However, the American plant was almost twice as productive as its U.K. rival. Why did this enormous difference in productivity occur? Several days of interviewing workers at all levels revealed striking differences.

The Americans demonstrated two simple attributes: professionalism and pride in the job. From floor sweeper to factory manager, each employee in the American plant regarded his or her job as something to be done really well. The floor sweeper spent his lunch break reading a copy of *Factory Sanitation Monthly*. This attitude was typical. Everyone interviewed showed a commitment to the job.

The British demonstrated different attitudes as they performed identical tasks. There was an air of sullen resentment in the factory. Decades of aggressive trade-union defensiveness had left its mark on management-union relationships. Management saw the work force as intransigent mules who needed coercion, while the work force acted as if they were the victims of relentless exploitation. Indifference and neglect caused many errors which were revealed in the productivity figures. A postscript to this study is that the British factory has now closed.

This study reveals that doing things right is an aspect of company culture — the system of values, beliefs, practices, attitudes, and habits which give an organization its special character. Accordingly, those in management have to manage the following key dimensions of company culture:

- Ensuring that managers share a common view of the organization's direction
- Awakening everyone to the nature of those competitive forces which are threats
- Monitoring values and beliefs at every level
- Putting money into climate change programs
- Making a senior manager responsible for integrating climate change activities

Those organizations that insist on high standards enjoy a well-motivated work force. Most people like to associate themselves with excellence and it becomes a source of personal pride. Care must be taken to ensure that the same standards are attained by all hierarchical levels. Gone are the days when the bosses could live a life of indolence, while employees were expected to behave like docile worker bees. The doing-things-right ethic must apply from top to bottom.

The five benefits of a doing-things-right culture are as follows:

1. Increased probability that corporate strategies will be successfully implemented
2. Easier integration of new technologies

3. Fewer damaging interdepartmental conflicts
4. More chance that employees will be positive
5. Higher customer satisfaction

Over the past decade, practical ways to do things right have been developed. For instance, at the work-group level, many organizations now use the quality-circles approach. At a typical quality-circle meeting, a group of workers comes together under the guidance of the supervisor to discuss concrete proposals for improving operations in the department. Apparently small matters, like the layout of components, are enthusiastically analyzed, discussed, and brainstormed. Detailed proposals emerge, and many of the ideas prove sound.

Quality circles are not a magic solution, and it takes a great deal of work to get them to work. Nevertheless, we need such concepts for restoring care in the workplace. Such techniques transform good intentions into action, without undermining the power structure of the organization.

Repeatedly we return to the topic of culture. All communities develop an identifiable character, which is a system of unwritten beliefs, conventions, and typical ways of behaving. New recruits absorb the prevailing values through a process known as socialization. All the individuals may change, but the culture lives on, almost as if the organization itself were a living thing. The behaviors that encourage a doing-things-right culture include these:

- Management personnel practicing what they preach
- Restructuring organizations into smaller units, to increase the sense of ownership
- Getting as many employees as possible to have contact with customers, so that they feel the impact of their work on others
- Reviewing the reward system to support the doing things right ethic.

- Giving "saturation" training to inculcate the desired values
- Using high-involvement techniques, like quality circles, to channel interest, tap creativity, increase care, and heighten commitment
- Establishing clear success criteria and monitoring performance

Planned programs to change organizational cultures have two potential enemies — cynicism from the bulk of employees and inadequate skills on the part of the managers. Most people who work in organizations have witnessed many attempts to enliven and focus corporate energies. Inevitably, they go along with the latest enthusiasms but inwardly bide their time, knowing that next month a new fad will emerge. The antidote to cynicism is dedicated managers who have personally committed themselves to change and have the skills to lead a change program. Superficial pronouncements of good intentions can make a negative impact; therefore, it is necessary to identify a few profound principles and hammer them home repeatedly. When actions support words, people begin to feel that "this is for real" and so cynicism slowly dissipates.

All the preceding thoughts occurred to us as we suffered that irritating flight. When the plane was somewhere over Greenland, we asked ourselves what we would do if this were our airline that was comprehensively mistreating us. We decided that there were four policies which we would adopt and that we would aggressively monitor their implementation. These are the policies:

1. To comprehensively train the leading flight attendants as team leaders and ensure that frequent retraining occurs
2. To insist that structured preflight meetings always take place so that the cabin crew is tuned in to the task
3. To collect feedback from a sample of customers from every flight, and insist that the crew discuss how to eliminate every reasonable negative observation

4. To check attitudes regularly among all the cabin crew to reduce the risk that there will be a buildup of lethargy or resentment

As we got off the plane, struggling past the crew members who were concerned only with their own last-minute packing, we realized, once again, that brilliant strategic business maneuvers are a small part of the managerial job. The secret is getting thousands of simple things done well, time and time again.

Three months after we started writing this chapter on that unpleasant flight, the final editing was done by one of the authors on a flight of another airline. What a contrast it was to the earlier flight. Nothing was too much trouble for the cabin staff; they did *everything* right, and never stopped smiling throughout the fifteen-hour flight. Next time that we have a choice about which airline we will fly, the decision will be obvious: Organizations that do things right get their customers back!

SUMMARY: CORE PRINCIPLES — DOING THINGS RIGHT

- The customer is the ultimate judge of whether you do things right.
- People see the world in different ways, but organizations need people to perform in similar ways.
- When social values do not support efficiency, then management must fight against the prevailing social trends.
- It is necessary to influence the "opinion leaders" at every level, since these are the people who largely determine standards.
- It is possible deliberately to develop and sustain a high-performing culture.
- Excessive bureaucracy undermines efficiency; as responsibility is taken away from the individual, so quality falls.

- Managers need to develop the skills of effective persuaders.
- Symbolic communication, what managers actually do, is more powerful than words.
- An organization can be destroyed when "doing things wrong" becomes part of the culture.
- People take pride in doing things well.
- Quality circles are an example of building a doing-things-right culture into work groups.
- Managers must practice what they preach.
- The secret is in getting many simple things done well, over and over again.

FIVE PRACTICAL STEPS TO ENCOURAGE DOING THINGS RIGHT

1. Set up two study groups with membership from several levels of your organization. Assign both groups the task of examining your most successful competitors to identify what is special about their ways of doing things. Tell the groups to work independently, to avoid the risk of "groupthink." If possible, the groups should visit the other organizations and examine their products, services, policies, practices, and so on. They should talk to customers. Each group should then be asked to conduct a three-hour workshop for the top team on their findings and ideas on ways to learn from your competitors.

2. Experiment with the quality-circles concept. Select keen and progressive middle managers, telling them to learn about the benefits and disadvantages of the application of quality circles. It is helpful to get an experienced consultant involved. Choose several promising work groups and apply the techniques. Carefully monitor the results. Avoid trying to extend the use of

the technique to other parts of your organization too quickly.

3. Ask your training department to obtain a copy of the film called *We Are on the Same Team, Remember*[3] (it is a superb technique for alerting people to the issues connected with doing things right). Get the trainers to propose how the film (or an alternative) could be used as part of an organizationwide campaign. The discussion-group technique is recommended. Experiment with the use of the film in selected parts of the organization.

4. Have a monthly "quality theme" which deals with an aspect of doing things right. Everyone in the organization should be blitzed with the need to deal with the particular issue. Use all the techniques of the advertising professionals. Ideas should be solicited from each level in the organization. A fully participative approach is best. Obtain feedback on the success of your communications, and keep refreshing the message.

5. Find ways for managers to learn about the topic of changing organization culture. Obtain input from academics, consultants, and managers who have experienced the process firsthand. There is much useful written material.* Experiment with techniques for measuring corporate culture. Try controlled experiments in changing culture and learn from the experience.

---

*See, for example, Schein, E. H. (1986). *Organizational Culture and Leadership*. San Francisco: Jossey-Bass.

REFERENCES

1. Weber, M. *The Protestant Ethic and the Spirit of Capitalism*, translated by Talcott Parsons (1986). New York: Counterpoint Paperbacks.
2. See Francis, D. (1987). *Unblocking Organizational Communication*, Chapter 5. Aldershot, Surrey, U.K.: Gower.
3. From Roundtable Films, 113 North Sanvicente Blvd., Beverly Hills, California 90211.

CHAPTER 9

Economy: No Free Lunches

It is a great deal easier to spend money than to make it. Lack of effective cost control is a common cause of business failure and organizational waste. The discipline rendered by the profit-and-loss account endows the wise commercial enterprise with the ultimate measure of success. Every activity costs money; some-one, somewhere has to pay. The successful organization under-stands the importance of facing economic reality. It adopts this value: *No free lunches.*

The entrepreneurs of the nineteenth century concerned themselves with old-fashioned virtues like balanced books, low borrowing, and real money. They asserted that everything had to be earned, or, to borrow Professor Friedman's expressive state-ment, "There is no such thing as a free lunch."[1]

This prudent philosophy was considered obsolete by many influential people by the 1950s when many decision makers be-came guided by the economic theories of John Maynard Keynes, who was one of the most original thinkers of the twentieth century. His prescriptions for national well-being included spend-ing one's way out of recession and stimulating economic activity by increasing consumption. Many economies implemented variants of Keynesian theory but experienced major problems, especially rampant inflation.

In recent years there has been a rise of alternative economic theories, which seek to remedy the practical weaknesses of Keynesian theory. Many of them owe their origins to the ideas of Adam Smith, who wrote in 1776 that ". . . every individual necessarily labors to render the annual revenue of the society as great as he can. He generally, indeed, neither intends to promote the public interest, nor knows he is promoting it. . . . he intends only his own gain, and he is in this as in many other cases, led by an invisible hand to promote an end that was no part of his intention. By pursuing his own interest he frequently promotes that of the society more effectually than when he really intends to promote it."[2] Adam Smith believed that when people freely pursue self-interest, they in fact contribute to national well-being. This economic viewpoint has been re-enlivened in the last twenty years, especially by the economist Milton Friedman, whose intellectual wisdom inspired managers in the 1970s to rediscover the fundamental truth in Mr. Micawber's dictum that "Annual income twenty pounds, annual expenditure nineteen pounds six, result happiness. Annual income twenty pounds, annual expenditure twenty pounds, nought and six, result misery."[3]

What has this to do with management? Of course, managers do not have to understand macroeconomics in detail, but their own economic theories affect their day-by-day decision making. An economic theory is a crucial part of the managerial value system.

The change in the prevailing economic philosophy from Keynesian to strict government control of money supply, known as monetarist, is a partial return to traditional prudent economic precepts, and it has influenced managers in several important ways.

Most of today's senior managers, who studied economics in the 1940s–1960s, were greatly influenced by the Keynesian tradition. Perhaps more importantly, in many countries they are (or were), in part, victims of government economic policies, which are profligate. The "softness" of Keynesianism permits an appeasing industrial-relations ethos to thrive. For example, in the 1970s, British management found itself unable to take prudent action, partly as a result of government-inspired spendthrift mentality.

Managers have been disadvantaged over the long term by the Keynesian economic stance which undermines the belief that we should pay ourselves only what we deserve and spend only what we earn. Unfortunately, a view of economics developed which suggested that governments could make the world prosperous simply by printing more money. This led to an unwarranted belief in the power of government and a lack of concern with the fundamental principle that only profit-and-loss accounts can measure commercial success.

The consequences of neglecting economic reality are illustrated by a personal example. Some years ago, both of the authors worked with an Industrial Training Board whose task was to encourage the development of human resources across a wide spectrum of British companies. We energetically took on this task. However, only after one of the authors left this now-defunct government agency to build his own business did he realize just how much money had been foolishly spent on trying to achieve training board objectives. The second author, an accountant and businessman, had constantly argued for economic prudence, but to no avail. It was routine to call people from all over the country for lengthy meetings; money was casually spent on staying in elegant hotels, and of course there was the usual annual scramble to spend surplus funds before the end of the financial year. In our work with the training board we probably made hundreds of direct and indirect decisions to spend money in ways which, if the cash had been ours, we would not have done. This was not a deliberately prodigal approach; indeed, from some viewpoints we were commendably careful, but the whole organization was driven by concerns other than value for money.

Such wasteful attitudes are often found in organizations which spend other people's money. They do not think about

Milton Friedman's insight that "there is no such thing as a free lunch," nor do they consider that when they spend so easily, they are diverting resources away from wealth creation.

One senior manager (responsible for a major company in New Zealand) put the matter clearly. She said, "The plain truth is that, whether we like it or not, we have to live and compete in world markets. Our national standard of living is dependent upon economic performance. In the end people will always choose to buy that which offers the best value for money, and it follows that those companies or countries which do not offer value for money will fail to prosper." This simple but profound argument needs to be universally appreciated.

The simple wisdom of this analysis is illustrated by a study of the British economy throughout the 1970s. Wages rose faster than output, thus fueling inflation. This increased the cost of goods and services, and the nation became increasingly uncompetitive. Industries in other countries took advantage of the weakness in the British economy; as a direct result, unemployment grew in the United Kingdom. With much pain and upheaval, many British firms went out of business. To mix our metaphors, all those free lunches came home to roost.

Managers, perhaps more than most categories of people, need to clarify their own values about economics. In the 1980s many governments, including the Soviet government, began to expose their industries to the shock of global commercial realities. There was a partial return to the values of a free-market economy. Where this was done, for example in the United Kingdom, for the first time in many years productivity began to improve significantly. The organizations which have adapted and survived are genuinely leaner and fitter. Twenty years of trying to be competitive through negotiation had largely failed. Direct exposure to the tyranny of the profit-and-loss account was much more successful. It is a fundamental belief of successful management's thinking that companies perform better when they are exposed to the forces of free competition. This discipline is irreplaceable.

Protectionism breeds weakness. An amusing example of this occurred when some major trades unions stopped using their "tied" printer (who had a permanent contract and did not need to bid for jobs) because they were simply uncompetitive; other printers could do the job faster, better, and cheaper. There are many such examples; refuse collection has been "privatized" by many local authorities, usually reducing the cost dramatically. Even the threat of "privatization" of public services often provokes major economies.

Commercial companies must be exposed to the principle of survival of the fittest. Such enterprises welcome the invigorating discipline of the capitalist economic system — which serves as a constant reminder that efficiency, effectiveness, and results are the fundamental criteria for judging performance.

The value system which underlies capitalism needs to be translated into a competitive and enterprising culture. Managers know deep in their bones that truths like Mr. Micawber's dictum are real. People in organizations must at all times be reminded that their concern needs to be "financially sound and commercially viable." Once preoccupation with economic viability is lost, any organization becomes perilously vulnerable. As many people have found to their cost, bankrupt organizations do not survive. Human and material resources are wasted when economic logic ceases to be the primary consideration. One manager made the point this way: "It is inhumane to manage badly or become uncompetitive. What human principle would this serve?"

The "no free lunches" principle is illustrated by the following example. The early months of a breakfast commercial television company, TV-am, demonstrated painfully that good ideas and a "vision" of the future are necessary, but are not sufficient, ingredients for success. Lord Marsh, as chairman of TV-am, described the first disastrous year this way: "That was probably where we failed as a board — we hadn't appointed a management team. There are seldom any villains in this kind of thing. I think that the biggest fault of those running it initially was simply a tendency not to see TV-am as a perfectly normal business which has to have financial controls, management information, cash flow forecasts—all the dull, dreary things which at the end of the day are what you succeed or fail by." New management had to "get the basic economics right," literally by cutting out those free lunches. Only then did TV-am begin to thrive. Later the new-found economic reality resulted in a highly successful flotation on the U.K. stock market. This success would never have been possible in the days of free lunches. We must conclude, therefore, that for individuals, companies, industries, or nations, the judgment of the marketplace is what really matters.

The antidote to economic myopia is stark exposure to commercial realities. This biological analogy is perfect: without well-balanced exercise and a proper diet, human beings degenerate into flabby and unhealthy specimens. Organizations grow stronger under a tough regime. The harsh, sometimes crude, discipline of commercial results is the only viable strategy for survival. The principle is that the more people are protected from the economic consequences of their actions, the more their long-term future is prejudiced.

The consequences of not using this "economic-realities"-driven management philosophy are severe as the following example shows. Between the two world wars, the British motorcycle industry was the world's premier producer. A "British bike" was a well-engineered, state-of-the-art "thoroughbred" offering excellent value for money. Success continued for a while after World War II; then Japanese manufacturers saw opportunities and swept the world market with their convenient, low-cost, excellent new-generation motorcycles. British producers initially reacted with a dogmatic rejection of the facts, claiming that the new fashions would be short-lived. Then they tried to compete, but it was too little, too late. Now, the British motorcycle industry is almost dead.

A manager friend who had worked in the British motorcycle industry commented, "Managers should step back from their day-by-day preoccupations and reflect upon the reasons for economic decline. What happens nationally is reflected in most organizations. It is both untruthful and wrong to blame work people alone for national weakness." Most people now accept that both management and workers enjoyed too many free lunches in the immediate post-war period. It does not pay to be soft and indulgent. In the authors' experience, there are winds of change blowing through the boardrooms in many countries. Managements must take much of the blame for the lack of commercial consciousness at every organizational level.

It will take time to flush away the corrosive psychological effects of Keynesian economics. A factory cleaner cannot be expected to respect the higher financial objectives of the boardroom unless these are described in ways that relate to his job and his world. What do millions of pounds, management ratios, and international currency fluctuations mean to him? The true answer is "a great deal," but too often those in top management fail to communicate this message effectively. The educational role is important to all managers. Messages must not be crude manipulative propaganda if they are to be credible. Persuasive communication is effective only when it is valid and truthful; unfortunately, though, managers are usually ill-trained in effective communication.

The marketplace offers an ever-present "university" that teaches what succeeds and what fails. We may not like the lessons, but they are real. Managers in successful organizations work to ensure that every member of the organization feels in contact with the marketplace. One example is the Volvo company, which ensures that when a car is returned with significant faults, the production team that built it see the results of their poor workmanship and put it right. Japanese businesspeople talk about taking the skin temperature of the customer each day. Such market consciousness, ideally, is promoted by insightful accountants who are required to get to know the firm's products, not to bury themselves in figures. As the chairman of a large company told us, "the aim must be to ensure that all become acutely aware of the real implications of today's economic environment. Otherwise we will all lose."

Economic factors are increasingly international, as shown by the destruction of the European zipper industry in the 1970s. The Japanese YKK company developed high-quality, low-cost machines which enabled them to become superb producers. After they entered Europe, the existing zipper manufacturing companies, once cozy in their protected havens, realized too late that it is insufficient to be just nationally competitive. Commercial realities operate on an international scale. Of course, this has profound implications for managers, who must seek out the most competent, comparable organizations anywhere in the world, and study them with the rapt attention that a cat gives to a mouse.

MANAGEMENT IMPLICATIONS

At a down-to-earth level, an economic preoccupation means that successful managers are committed to an attitude of "good husbandry." Jobs are examined to discover what potential influence the individual can have over economic performance, and these variables are measured, recorded, and regularly reviewed. Increasingly, computer systems make it possible to give rapid feedback to job holders. Even in noncommercial fields this can be done. For example, in many countries doctors get feedback on the costs involved in meeting their prescriptions for drugs, and can use this information to give value for money.

Unfortunately, measurements and feedback are often the responsibility of experts who, in our experience, are usually primarily concerned with meeting legal and system requirements. Thus they fail to contribute fully their professional skills to increasing commercial awareness and promoting better systems for giving key financial data to those who can use the information. After all, one good reason for reviewing the past is to change future behavior.

Although commercial success is fundamental, it is not always supreme. Sometimes more profound principles are at stake.

The first draft of this chapter was written during the 1984 siege of the Libyan Embassy, which began with the barbaric murder of a young policewoman. Britain decided to sever diplomatic relations with Libya, causing Britain to lose many millions of pounds in exports. Yet, there was no alternative; basic morality is more important than commercial self-interest. Principles of international law and order must be maintained whatever the cost. Decision makers must distinguish between moral and immoral profitability.

Commercial logic requires that long-term interests are not sacrificed for short-term gain. The insistent demands of monthly and annual high targets tend to focus managers' minds on the immediate, not the long, term. Profitability today may disguise potential weakness tomorrow. Successful managers are committed to permanence and make prudent investments which pay off years later. They try to balance profit today with investment in the future. That contributes to the long-term benefit of shareholders, employees, and the community.

SUMMARY: CORE PRINCIPLES — NO FREE LUNCHES

- Economic values are a crucial part of the organization's value system.
- Managers often need to clarify their own economic values.
- Monetarist economic theories provide the most useful economic model for managers in commercial companies.
- We should pay ourselves only what we deserve and spend only what we earn.
- Organizations thrive best when they are children of capitalism.
- Governments cannot remedy all economic weaknesses.
- Noncommercial organizations are especially vulnerable to forgetting the no-free-lunch principle.

- Every employee must be concerned with profit and loss.
- Direct exposure to economic reality is the best way to get an organization lean and fit.
- Great efforts have to be made to ensure that employees understand the economic results of their work.
- Jobs should be described in ways that focus on the economic consequences of success and failure.
- Specialist managers should receive training to help them to understand the impact of their specialism on the organization as a whole.
- Sometimes deeper issues, like the maintenance of law and order, override economic considerations.
- Long-term economic viability must be built without sacrificing short-term profitability.

FIVE PRACTICAL STEPS TO ENCOURAGE THE NO-FREE-LUNCHES VALUE

1. Ask each senior manager to prepare a written answer to the question: "Imagine you owned this organization — what would you do differently?" Compile an overview of the suggestions made for top management review and action planning.
2. Arrange for your trade union representatives to receive business-school training in the financial aspects of management. Ensure that they are aware of the economic impact of wage rates and labor restrictions on productivity. Find ways for your trade union representatives to examine competitors' finances both at home and abroad.
3. Ask every manager to identify ways in which his or her department or unit adds value to products or services. These can be boldly written on a poster displayed in the workplace and constantly reviewed. Enlist the help of

computer consultants to discover how you can supply more immediate and graphic information on productivity to those immediately concerned.

4. Give all supervisors and managers company/unit accounts and help them to understand the implications. If necessary, special training programs should be conducted. Then each manager or supervisor discusses the implications with members of her or his own team, and they, in turn, cascade such discussions down through the organization.

5. Obtain comparative statistics on the profitability and productivity of your part of the organization compared with similar ones in the United States, Japan, and Europe. (Such information is often obtainable from trade or industry associations). Make the information widely available and discuss it across the organization. Form action groups to remedy identified weaknesses.

REFERENCES

1. Friedman, M. (1981). *Capitalism and Freedom*. Chicago: University of Chicago Press.
2. Smith, A. (1922). *An Inquiry into the Nature and Power of the Wealth of Nations*. Edited by E. Carran. New York: Methuen, p. 423.
3. Dickens, C. *David Copperfield*. (1981). Oxford, U.K.: Oxford University Press.

Managing Relationships

CHAPTER 10

Fairness: Who Cares Wins

One of the greatest compliments paid to a good teacher is that he or she is "firm but fair." Managements, by their actions, greatly affect people's lives, both in work and outside. What they do, and what they refuse to do, has a major impact on the quality of life of all employees. Using this power with compassion and fairness builds trust and commitment. The successful organization realizes that peoples' views, perceptions, and feelings are important. It adopts this value: *Who cares wins*.

Throughout the centuries, enlightened businessmen and businesswomen have accepted a moral responsibility to run organizations in ways that enable individuals to thrive. Managerial power shapes the destiny of all those who work in the organization, and the most successful industrialists care for both people and profit. In the early twentieth century this stance evolved into a definite management philosophy, known as *paternalism*, which advocates that those in control of organizations should behave like "good fathers."

Paternalism was not to last: after World War II, coincidental with the expansion of trade union power and the welfare state, paternalism became derided as a wasteful and soft-headed philosophy which disregarded current realities and was considered to be essentially humiliating to employees.

Paternalism is "the principle and practice of paternal administration: government as by a father" (*Shorter Oxford Dictionary*). There are, of course, many variations of the paternal role. The proper role of a father is to provide whatever is needed to bring the child to responsible adulthood. This requires firmness and understanding, discipline and freedom. Fathers give both support and direction. In return, they receive loyalty and love.

It was a shame that paternalism became so unfashionable. For several decades after World War II, trade unions in many countries attracted almost unquestioned loyalty, and many employers were cast in the role of the enemy. Such social divisions proved very destructive. Workers, who are usually dependent on the organization that employs them, are greatly affected by decisions made far above them. What is wrong with decision-makers recognizing that they are partly responsible for the interests of their employees?

To take the argument further, consider how managerial power is used. All large organizations centralize strategic decision-making in the hands of relatively few people who become an elite. Top managers can devise effective systems for collecting information, making choices, and allocating resources. Most commercial organizations in the western world use ownership as the principle on which power is distributed. Noncommercial organizations (like local government) use democratically elected groups to perform the same role. Whatever approach is used, the result is the same; a small group directs the fortunes of the whole. The ruling elite invariably operate with an explicit or implicit code of morality or immorality.

Some top managements, from our observation, pay scant attention to their paternal responsibilities, yet they take considerable care in technical analysis. Markets are studied, graphs drawn, strategies evaluated, and opportunities carefully weighed.

A considerable amount of expertise is invested in strategic decisions, but little time is spent on considering human issues. Such top managers take every possible precaution to avoid undue risks. They try to invest in ventures with a high probability of profit. However, emphasis on short-term return on investment to the exclusion of other criteria is contrary to the principles of paternalism. Human interests, beginning with material prosperity, are the primary goals. As we have said many times throughout this book, mere materialism is a shallow philosophy.

Once managers begin to consider the morality of their decisions, they usually become more paternalistic. The best of them show enormous care for their employees but are never soft. Paternalism requires surveillance and watchfulness. Employees are helped and guided to improve their performance. Demands are made and standards set. Increasing competence earns increasing recognition.

The main danger for paternalistic managers is that they can get out of touch. Because they assume that they know what is good for others, communication difficulties often occur. Such problems are not inevitable, though; if the right degree of watchfulness is maintained, then paternalism does not have to result in psychological isolation.

Behaving like a good father may seem opposed to the principles of individualism and self-reliance. Not so! The individual freely decides that he or she will strike a bargain with an employer. Organizations, in effect, then demand that employees abandon some of the responsibility for their own destiny, but individual workers have made a free choice to put their well-being partly in the hands of someone else. Once this decision is made, the individual has invested in the fortunes of a corporate body and has a right to expect that this trust will be reciprocated.

Fortunately, paternalism is not dead. It is undergoing a renaissance and has arisen again under different guises. For example, many American companies have instituted a policy of "social responsibility." Major Japanese firms, which are teaching us much about the effective use of resources, adopt employee philosophies which support the individual through thick and thin. Many European companies are reflecting anew on business ethics. This is a new-style paternalism which accepts that organizations have a moral responsibility for the consequences of managerial decisions.

It is difficult to capture in words the subtle blend of boldness and caution which typifies the caring stance. For an explanation we can borrow an idea from a great industrialist. Thomas Watson of IBM recognized the fundamental importance of solid beliefs in organizational success. He wrote, "Consider any great organization that has lasted over the years, and I think you will find that it owed its resilience not to its form of organization or administrative skills, but to the power of what we call beliefs and the appeal these beliefs provide. This, then, is my thesis: I firmly believe that any organization, in order to survive and achieve success, must have a sound set of beliefs on which it premises all its policies and actions. Next, I believe that the most important single factor in the corporate success is faithful adherence to those beliefs. And finally, I believe that if an organization is to meet the challenges of a changing world, it must be prepared to change everything about itself except those beliefs as it moves through corporate life."[1] A number of industrialists have understood the importance of moral leadership. Sir John Egan described his period as managing director of Jaguar cars in the following way: "Overall we have tried to create an environment at Jaguar which is the exact opposite of the purely instrumental approach which characterizes the employee's attitude to his company in so much of industry. We know the dividends this pays, not only in terms of generating a much better atmosphere within our factories but also in our people's willingness to go far beyond the normal call of duty when problems arise." The Jaguar approach paid off — productivity trebled between 1980 and 1984, and industrial stoppages fell from 800,000 employee hours to less than 5,000 hours.[2]

Opponents claim that paternalism inevitably generates dependency, and so damages personal initiative and self-responsibility. Moreover, it is argued that paternalism is expensive and inevitably leads to an unacceptable tolerance of inefficiency. The antipaternalists argue that fair wages are sufficient reward for effort, and that providing any more erodes managerial discretion, blunts the competitive edge, and binds workers to organizations for negative reasons.

Paternalism is a hazardous management philosophy because it can degenerate into a soft and weak stance if the commitment to high standards is lacking. That which is given from an enlightened and compassionate attitude may be seen as "something for nothing." If they support unacceptable behavior managers store up trouble ahead. However, if they can walk the tightrope, then paternalism is positive and morally defensible and therefore justifies a relentless drive towards productivity.

Well-managed paternalism evokes loyalty. Some of the most successful organizations thrive because they possess a strong ideology which includes a caring philosophy towards people. This ideology may arise either from the vision of one person or from a succession of episodes of distinguished endeavor evolved into a historic identity.

Caring like a good father also has implications for the role business plays in the wider community. In an address to the Institute of Directors, the Prince of Wales drew attention to a neglected facet of business values — responsibility to the community as a whole. Prince Charles pointed out that business naturally exploited "rich pickings" and so neglected the poorer areas of society. This meant that socially deprived areas degenerated further, both materially and morally. Large companies tended to suck wealth out of rundown communities and give little in return. He argued that owners and managers should maintain financial viability but use part of their power and wealth with the attitude of a good parent to help society as a whole. Such philanthropic attitudes are part of the caring tradition. They are not pie in the sky either. For example, in Brixton, South London, new community enterprises are thriving, funded in part by big business. In Mike Woodcock's constituency (Ellesmere Port and Westen), many new businesses have been helped to grow by assistance from large, established firms. Much more, however, needs to be done.

CARING MANAGEMENT

The rediscovery of caring principles is fashionable in the United States, where some management opinion leaders have discovered the importance of *meaning* and *purposes*, indicating the need for organizations to have a "heart" and to express human values. Purely rational strategies and concentration on profit are seen as necessary, but insufficient, motivators. Instead, organizations should be regarded as growing organisms which need a clear sense of purpose. While such management philosophies are considered as novel and extraordinary, they are really updated variations of paternalistic themes which have long been understood by the best industrialists and leaders.

Managers who deliberately abandon principles are actually operating on the principle that they have no principles. Organizations likewise operate from principles whether these have been articulated or not. They trade in certain ways and not others, treat their employees according to a definite philosophy, and promote some activities rather than others.

A coherent set of principles is a source of strength because

- Decisions are firmer.
- A consistent approach is adopted.
- Issues can be judged more quickly.
- Important "crunch points" can be readily identified.
- Others respect a principled stance.
- Trust is built.

Those who manage without a sound foundation of principles are weak or untrustworthy. In a crisis the unprincipled person tends to react to immediate pressures and to make bad decisions which have ramifications for many years.

Principles can be clarified by these four steps:

1. *Decide to be honest.* Only by examining how you really think and feel (not how you *should*) can genuine principles be uncovered.
2. *Express your current views.* Allowing yourself to freely express your views reveals what your stance really is.
3. *Consider alternatives.* Develop the capacity to open your mind to other views.
4. *Write down your principles.* This process helps you clarify and, equally important, test whether your principles are consistent with one another.

Often people say one thing but do another. Such inconsistency is important, and should be explored. The way you actually behave is a more lucid statement of your principles than your rhetoric. It is often helpful to discuss and debate principles with others. Reasonable and factual argument is a great antidote to prejudice and bigotry. Moreover, it is valuable to gather viewpoints from people whose stance is very different from your own.

Caring managers know their principles and seek to put them into effect. Accomplishing this is difficult, because principles are ephemeral things, difficult to grasp and hard to consider. As managers discuss their principles concerning the treatment of people, they may find themselves paying lip service to principles which they never put into practice. Principles must be simple and explicit, and then carried out.

Harvey-Jones, former chairman of ICI (Imperial Chemical Industries), believes that the most effective organizations are those in which the values of the organization support the values of the individual, and vice versa. He said, "You cannot, in industry, work totally on the principle that the end justifies the means. The ends have to be felt to be good, and the ethics of the organization, i.e., how it behaves in pursuit of its ends, have to be seen as decent and in tune with the times." Harvey-Jones was amazed that ethics was only an optional extra at the Harvard Business School.[3] Business schools pay scant regard to ethics, values, and principles.* Without these topics being seriously studied in the upper echelons of business education, it is not surprising that few senior managers can describe a coherent set of caring principles.

Many organizations of the left, for example, the Co-operative Movement, have a distinguished record of implementing paternalistic policies if not of commercial success. The distinctive element of productive paternalism is the 'contractual' principle on which it is based. Expressed simply this says 'We will care for you if you give us what we want!' Paternalism should be demanding as well as giving.

The right-wing view of paternalism is akin to that of the good father whose support is strong but conditional; the child is cared for within limits but encouraged to take responsibility for himself or herself whenever possible. The socialist concept of paternalism is more like that of the mother, with unconditional support no matter what the child does. We accept that total care for infants is both necessary and desirable. Adults, however, thrive poorly in totally benign environments. Personal initiative, which needs to be developed, withers without use. Accounts of prison camps vividly illustrate that the capacity of prisoners to make decisions deteriorates if it cannot be used. Mothering of adults is a stultifying process that erodes individual dignity.

Managers must be realists; they know that many people develop a degree of dependence on their employer, which often

---

*Things are changing, however. In 1987 Harvard Business School received a $30 million grant to establish an ethics course. See Harvey-Jones, J. (1988). *Making It Happen: Reflections on Leadership*. London: Collins.

suits managers who require most employees to play significant but highly limited roles. Dependency is a dangerous relationship for the dependent person. There is a strong probability that people will find themselves in difficulties. Illness or family problems occur and, most common these days, jobs are radically changed or rendered obsolete. Top managers in a large conglomerate, in deciding to restructure a nationwide business, remove from the map a small dot representing a branch office. This is a relatively trivial matter for the executives but has dramatic consequences for those affected.

The roles of father and mother carry powerful emotional undertones. The paternal figure often triggers hostile reactions. Traditional authoritarian behavior tends to evoke childlike responses such as passive compliance or loud, aggressive resistance. Neither response is constructive. "Acting superior" with a judgmental and punitive style is often provocative. The manner of expression is as powerful as a physical act.

Despite the difficulties of expression, we cannot avoid observing that great organizations are often led by caring managers who are great paternalists. They succeed because their employees work well for them. The best situation for managers is to have a fiercely loyal and high-performing work force. Management gains points by helping those who are disadvantaged, rewarding loyalty, enriching the quality of working life, and doing everything possible to be a good employer.

As part of our preparation for this book, we asked twenty-three long-established chairmen of successful companies about their decision-making styles. Some common features that emerged are as follows:

- Ensuring that they had an objective assessment of the strengths and weaknesses of their own businesses
- Clarifying what factors gave the organization its distinctive character
- Discovering what members of the organization feel proud of achieving

- Encouraging objective analysis and critique of the present organization
- Demonstrating that they are prepared to listen
- Honoring the history of their organization
- Seeking out and unblocking areas of the organization which have degenerated
- Exercising caution in introducing new ideas
- Explaining fully their reasoning on important decisions
- Avoiding a condescending attitude toward the work force

Making a bargain is the essence of the paternal relationship. Lord Bancroft, former head of the Home Civil Service, helped us understand the fundamental importance of a contract between management and staff. He said, "A management's deeds and words should approximate each other. It is all very well to tell staff that management will strike a bargain; that in return for efficiency, effectiveness, and economy, it will encourage and care for its employees. Both sides must keep to any implicit or explicit bargain." Books on child care tell us that the young require consistency from their parents: employees are entitled to expect integrity from their bosses.

BENEFITS OF PATERNALISM

Paternalism can be supported for these six reasons:

- Organizations earn high commitment from employees by showing high commitment to them.
- The management's right to manage is enhanced by an obviously responsible stance.
- People are more likely to trust a good employer.
- In a competitive job market, respected employers attract the best recruits.
- Managers feel more able to take a "firmer" approach to

managing change if they know possible damage to people will be minimized.

- Paternalism undermines destructive social class barriers and weakens the power base of militant trade unions.

New-style paternalism, which is clearly different from the pompous superiority typical of the Victorian mill owner, is persuasive rather than oppressive. All possible mechanisms for persuasion are used to communicate with the work force. There is an interesting analogy with computers, which have recently become "user-friendly." This means that the computer is approachable, communicates in language that the user can understand, and appears to adopt a considerate attitude. Managements are learning to become "user-friendly" in the same way. This approach does not reduce the paternal responsibilities of management, but it does make the form of expression a contemporary one.

Another dimension of caring is the concern for stable human communities. Organizations depend on communities, and people depend on organizations; the relationship is mutual interdependence. Managers can support communities in several ways:

- *Direct economic support*: through gifts, endowments, sponsorships, trusts, etc.
- *Indirect economic support*: by encouraging wealth creation
- *Managerial support*: by providing brainpower and expertise to community programs
- *Educational support*: by allowing the organization to welcome and help students and visitors
- *Political support*: by encouraging and funding political representatives whose philosophy is congenial
- *Resource support*: by assisting in community projects by donating resources

Caring managers have a tradition of being community-oriented; a proportion of corporate wealth is often allocated to community benefit. They take care to see that expenditure of time and money is afforded as "businesses can be responsible only if they are profitable." Yet managers must ask, "Profit for what?" One colleague put it this way: "Pursuing profit, for its own sake, is rooted in the shallow motivation of a miser, and gives a woefully inadequate base to build successful organizations. Profitability is the primary goal as it permits people to lead lives with choice and richness, but it is not an end in itself."

A company chairman, who built a large and successful enterprise, candidly stated his personal philosophy: "I feel a commitment to my organization which is akin to love. I have a great regard for the business and the people who work there. I am unwilling to be parted from my organization, and I feel a great pride in its achievements. I have been accused of being addicted to my company. The depth of emotion I feel has never been a weakness as people respond. I believe that organizations need a heart, and I am prepared to play this role." This man's view may seem naive and old-fashioned, but, in fact, it is ahead of its time. Feeling and heart are keys to successful management.

SUMMARY: CORE PRINCIPLES — WHO CARES WINS

- Paternalistic approaches have been mistakenly condemned as old-fashioned.
- American social responsibility and Japanese employee policies have much to teach European managers.
- Organizations which demand high productivity and loyalty should look after employees in return.
- Paternalism should be conditional and demanding, not soft and all-embracing.
- Managers who skillfully adopt paternalistic attitudes are enhancing their right to manage.
- Many highly effective and profitable companies thrive on a policy of paternalism.

- Paternalism must not be expressed as crude authoritarianism.
- Managements must become more skillful at communicating the benefits of a high-give/high-take relationship.

FIVE PRACTICAL STEPS TO ENCOURAGE THE WHO-CARES-WINS VALUE

1. Visit some Japanese organizations and talk to the employees about how management operates. Compare and contrast their attitudes with your own. Produce a report for top management discussion, and set up working parties to implement any changes which seem desirable.
2. Write down how you personally would like to be treated as an employee in any organization. Then go into your own organization to determine whether your conditions are operating in your organization. After identifying gaps, forcefully bring them to the attention of those who can take action.
3. Invite an industrial psychologist who specializes in attitude surveys to give a presentation on methods of collecting valid data on employee attitudes. Consider collecting such information regularly to determine how employees view the management of your organization. Alternatively, use the Blockage Survey[4] which is a systematic way of collecting valuable data about how an organization is functioning.
4. Informally discuss your managerial stance toward people with trade union officials. Encourage your senior managers to study trade-union literature. Research trade-union viewpoints to use in challenging your thinking. Keep in touch with evolving thinking in successful rival institutions.

5. Organize discussion groups of five employees chosen at random and invite them to discuss whether the company is a good employer. After obtaining their permission, tape-record the discussion and use the resulting analysis to encourage top management to debate whether the company is too soft, too hard, or just right.

REFERENCES

1. Watson, T. Jr. (1963). *A Business and Its Beliefs: The Ideas That Helped Build IBM.* New York: McGraw-Hill.
2. *Personnel Management,* (1984 April). London: Institute of Personnel Management.
3. Ibid., 10.
4. Smith, A. (1922). *An Inquiry into the Nature and Power of the Wealth of Nations.* Edited by E. Carran. New York: Methuen, p. 423.

Teamwork: Pulling Together

A well-organized and well-motivated group can achieve more than the sum of the individuals who comprise the group. People enjoy the company of others and can work well collectively. One person's talents can balance the weaknesses of another. It is vitally important that people feel that they belong. The successful organization ensures that it derives the benefits of effective teamwork. It adopts this value: *Pulling together.*

Studies of the excellence of particular organizations capture the imagination of managers. Case studies provided at management seminars encapsulate the attributes of the best organizations. The following summarizes many such presentations attended by the authors.

> Outstanding organizations are dynamic, energetic, focused, wisely led, and opportunistic. The people who work in such an organization really care about the quality of their work. The atmosphere is one of optimism, commitment, and high energy.

> This kind of organization will be capable of changing every-
> thing but its basic values. High achievement and the thesis of
> excellence are programmed into the minds of employees.

These are seen as the characteristics of excellent organizations whether they sell hamburgers or gather taxes. Their success
recipes are predictable but ephemeral. Moreover, the best organizations engender the same positive qualities that close and
happy families enjoy. We encourage organizations to try to
incorporate the value of family life, thereby providing a structure
on which to build constructive human relationships.

The Russian novelist Tolstoy said, "All happy families
resemble one another, but each unhappy family is unhappy in its
own way,"[1] emphasizing that a well-conducted family, like an
excellent organization, is good at getting the basics right.

It is interesting that senior managers often think about their
organization as an extension of their own family. Families are the
enduring units in human society, which provide roots that con-
nect people with past and future. Families provide identity and
give support to the family members. At their best, they are loved
and loyally protected. Of course, we must not be excessively
romantic. Some families are disturbed, unhappy, tyrannical and
damaging. However, few people would disagree that a soundly
based family is a powerful source for the good.

Promoting family life is an age-old value. Our forefathers,
who saw the family as an honorable and indispensable unit of
society, were cautious about tampering with such a natural
phenomenon.

In the twentieth century, traditional family structure has
come under threat. For example, the communist movement in
Russia was influenced by Karl Marx's condemnation of the
family,[2] which he believed to be an embodiment of the vices of
the exploiting class. The rise of feminism added to the growing
rebellion against traditional family structure. Radicals of various
persuasions have advocated the demise of the family, sometimes

visualizing the family as the seedbed of pathological and mental illness. We disagree, believing that closeness, kinship, support, honesty, and loyalty are all attributes of a good family.

Sometimes managers have been slow to recognize the value of thinking of their organizations as family groups. For example, many perceive employees as mere units of labor, giving scant recognition to their social and emotional needs. People in general are aware of the importance of forming close bonds in small groups. They naturally form teams, which act as "work families," and these groups become very important in their lives.

Teams are powerful and potent tools; they get people to the moon, audit complex accounts, make cinematic blockbusters, and run companies. Efficient teamwork provides these five major advantages:

- Individual weaknesses are neutralised by others' strengths.
- Teamwork builds consensus and commitment.
- Membership is a strong motivator.
- Teams discipline errant members.
- Errors and inattention are less likely to occur.

The team approach can satisfy both individual and corporate needs. Combined talents and skills achieve success where lone individuals would fail. Also, the well-devised team, like a healthy family, is an exceptional source of support and motivation, stimulating its members to excel.

It is useful to distinguish between the types of teams and their main roles as commonly found in organizations:

Top Teams: Provide direction, control and identity at the apex of the organization.

Management Teams: Devise, coordinate and control operational strategies and plans

Project Teams: Undertake specific assignments on "one-off" tasks

Creative Teams: Pool different talents to devise innovative solutions and seize opportunities

Work Teams: Communicate and co-operate to get jobs done

One of the first demonstrations of the importance of teams resulted from a study conducted shortly after World War II when techniques of coal mining in Britain were being radically changed. New mechanized equipment made less appropriate the traditional "informal family" teamwork required by hand mining. In the dark, dangerous underground conditions, isolated miners were suddenly asked to play fragmented new roles tending the "long-wall" machines. In effect, their work family was destroyed and informal communication inhibited. The result was low motivation, poor morale, and aggressive defensiveness. Researchers from the Tavistock Institute[3] suggested that teamwork be reestablished; after this was done, the social problems were gradually solved.

During the 1970s some established companies experimented with new forms of work organization that attempted to encourage responsible attitudes in the belief that improved productivity would result. They argued that the routine of organizational life reduced people to machines and close relationships were destroyed by the factory system. Because the workers were deprived of choice, it was not surprising that disinterest and irresponsible behavior flourished. Companies like United Biscuits, General Foods, and Imperial Chemical Industries tried to increase responsibility at shop floor level. In 1975 one of the authors visited a dog food factory owned by General Foods in Topeka, Kansas, and studied a highly productive and profitable unit that was largely organized by teams of operators led by a supervisor. Careful selection of personnel followed by intensive training enabled managers to assign almost all routine decision making to these groups. Responsibility was actually passed to those who were close to the action, and both workers and company shareholders gained.

Unfortunately, such experiments have proved the exception rather than the rule. Awareness of the importance of "family life" has been lost by many senior managers whose concerns are largely expressed in rows and numbers. Large organizations continue to create jobs that offer little discretion. It is not surprising that when genuine responsibility is absent, responsible behavior is also lacking.

Although there have been many demonstrations of the value of team building, it is not the panacea for solving all organizational problems. Some individuals are self-sustaining, and, for them, teamwork is inappropriate. Even where teamwork is desirable, it requires an open, communicating management style which not all managers are able or willing to use. Also, work families can turn against the wider organization.

Many managers are skeptical of the use of management by committee, which they feel undermines individuality and weakens responsibility. They recognize that they must exploit the potential of groups but they watch for the disadvantages. Groups and committees can muddy decision making, undermine individual self-confidence, and reduce people's contributions to the lowest common denominator. Unless well constructed, such groups can become satisfied with low-quality performance and waste an extraordinary amount of time in socializing. Some senior managers, noticing this tendency, understandably sound a note of caution about the teamwork approach. For example, Peter Walters, Chairman of British Petroleum, said of the team approach, "That was just one part of the personnel management claptrap which became the vogue in the 1960s. The truth was that one chap set the tone."[4]

Ironically, the strengths of "family relationships" mean that a team approach has proved a source of weakness in senior decision making. Some ideas developed by Professor Janus,[5] introduced in Chapter 7, are relevant. In a provocative study, he found that while some team decisions are outstandingly successful, there are unfortunately many examples of collective decision making which proved disastrous. His analysis of famous fiascos revealed that the team responsible committed one or more of the following blunders:

- Their discussions did not survey all of the available options.
- The original decision was not reevaluated for nonobvious drawbacks.
- Discarded options were not reexamined for nonobvious gains.
- Expertise was ignored because of the bias of powerful group members.
- Insufficient consideration was given to the reaction of outside groups.

Teams which operate like close and cohesive families are vulnerable to committing such blunders. The group develops an isolated approach and becomes almost a law unto itself. This is what Professor Janus calls *groupthink*. The symptoms are the following:

- Illusion of invulnerability feeds excessive optimism.
- Warnings are discounted.
- Ethical standards slip as the group becomes judge and jury.
- Other groups are considered inferior.
- Self-censorship prevents the expression of critical opinions within the team.
- Adverse information is ignored because it might shatter illusions.

The best teams are motivating and resourceful, but leaders have to be careful to avoid the dangers of groupthink. This requires the following:

- A norm must be established in the group of supporting, rather than punishing, divergent comments.
- Systematic decision-making disciplines should be understood and rigorously applied.

- Outside views should be collected to provide a check on the validity of decision making.

The authors' experience confirms the analysis of Professor Janus. Underdeveloped teams are managerially incompetent, and even developed teams must be used with care. Nevertheless, over the past decade we have become increasingly aware of the flexibility and power of the family-style team.

When teams have been carefully selected, insightfully led, and deliberately developed, they are a force for good. The value of the team approach for top management is emphasized by the Institute of Directors (an influential British organization that represents directors of private and public companies) which says, "Although a private company may, in law, have one director only, it would be in general unwise to do so. The reason for this lies in the nature of the decisions directors take. Based as they are on uncertain assumptions about the future, they require the exercise of a great deal of judgment and mental weighing and testing. No more efficient method has yet been discovered for carrying out this process than discussion by a well-informed small group.[6] One is reminded of a family group discussing an important problem together and collectively coming to a resolution.

Managers should remember that people need to feel a sense of ownership in their environment. This truth is illustrated in a production facility at Christmastime when workers exchange hundreds of cards and messages. These are often festooned around the machines. People need to make their mark on a small piece of their environment; this can be facilitated in the following ways:

- Asking people what they think about their working environment
- Acting to make appropriate changes in the working environment
- Providing the opportunity for each person to have some personal space

- Trying to humanize and individualize the environment (and not letting the ideas of external designers go unquestioned)
- Trying to ensure that people feel ownership of what they produce (through personal identification)

TEAM CONSTRUCTION

Over the past decade, managers have realized that it is both practical and desirable deliberately to select and build effective teams. Both of the authors have published practical guides to team building,[7] which describe how a disparate collection of individuals can learn to operate as a cohesive and effective team.

The initial challenge is to choose the appropriate ingredients. Like a good cook, the team designer should use a planned approach to find the best balance of personal skills and professional disciplines.

Some brilliant research by the British management developer, Dr. Meredith Belbin,[8] helps us understand how to construct a successful team. Teamwork requires a careful blend of ingredients. Simplifying Dr. Belbin's analysis, we find that effective teams contain people capable of performing the following roles:

- **Mr. Dutiful,** who works for the good of the company, is conservative and predictable.
- **Mr. Chairman,** who sets objectives and exploits everyone's best abilities.
- **Mr. Get-up-and-go,** who challenges, drives, and stimulates.
- **Mr. Ideas,** who uses imagination and proposes new ways to get things done.
- **Mr. Fix-it,** who knows people and explores situations.
- **Mr. Ponder,** who carefully weighs options before judging.
- **Mr. Harmony,** who bridges differences and makes people feel at home.

- **Mr. Get-the-job-done-right,** who ensures that tasks are finished to a high standard.

The successful manager will take great care to collect a complete mix of individuals in a well-balanced team. This provides a durable resource of stimulating and energetic people whose talents complement each other. Slowly, through a deliberate process of team building, these people become a work family.

TEAM BUILDING

Steps should be taken to weld the disparate group of individuals into a close-working group. This process requires the following:

1. A team manager who wishes to use a team approach
2. A group which has objectives that require them to work together
3. The basic willingness and skills for team working

When these conditions are present, the group becomes a suitable case for team building. Work relationships and real-life performance of tasks must be addressed, and team building focused on improving operational performance.

Just as families thrive on openness, so team building requires that each team member stand back and frankly evaluate how the team is operating as a working family. Inevitably, shortcomings will be exposed, so the team manager, who is in the "parent role," is in a vulnerable position. Much team building takes place informally, but we have found it is often helpful to have a two- or three-day team meeting devoted to improving performance. It takes leadership courage to begin. The team manager must understand what is about to happen and then agree to the process.

Managers sometimes use the services of a team-building consultant as an adviser to the whole team, not just to the team manager. This helps identify blockages to effectiveness, specify roles, review current practice, and plan how to improve. Just as families get locked into the status quo, so work teams can become insular. To offset this tendency, often team builders conduct a private "sensing interview" with each member of the team. This typically lasts for about one-and-a-half hours. What is said is considered anonymous but not confidential. Copious notes are taken, often of verbatim quotations. The consultant methodically collects data on matters such as the values of the team, its mission in the organization, goal clarity and commitment, relationships and accountability, decision-making processes and communication, leadership style and rewards, openness and trust, cooperation and competition, and relationships with other teams.

Recurrent themes always emerge. The consultant can use the experience to identify and categorize data under relevant headings. Care should be taken to ensure that comments cannot be traced to the person who made them. No attempt is made to interpret the results; the consultant's only task is accurately to present a "snapshot" of the team.

Categorized data are then presented to the team manager in a private coaching session. Several hours of discussion are usually required for the team manager to absorb the data and plan how to use them. The team-building session which follows is led by the existing team manager (**not** by the consultant, since this would undermine the integrity of the family). It is imperative that the team manager adopts a constructive role. Extensive discussion of the issues and guidance from the consultant enables the team-building session to be planned and conducted properly.

Then all team members meet off site. A country hotel is ideal as it provokes the development of family style relationships. We have found that a useful time frame is for team building to begin after work one evening and conclude at dinnertime on the third day. This gives two complete days of work, which is usually needed for an adequate review of team functioning.

The team off-site meeting can begin with an introduction by the team manager, who invites the consultant to share the data from the sensing interviews. All the information should be preentered on flip charts under appropriate headings. The consultant clarifies comments as he or she knew the context in which they were said. At this stage the team absorbs the information. When the consultant has finished displaying the data, the leader resumes charge of the meeting and in cooperation with other members of the team prepares the agenda. Normally this occupies the first evening.

The subsequent two days are spent methodically working through the agenda. As the team leader manages the sessions, action points emerge. These are recorded with responsibilities allocated. The consultant's task is to facilitate by helping the team address issues, directing attention to how the team is operating, giving short inputs on concepts or techniques, and suggesting mechanisms for improvement. It is important to ensure that the integrity of the work family is never undermined.

At the end of the session, the team has reviewed its operating effectiveness and devised an action plan for improvement. By addressing practical problems and opportunities collaboratively, the team evolves as a family work group and becomes a competent resource. It devises new ways of creatively working together in the future.

Just as families need to be sustained, so do teams. It is helpful to hold a review session a few weeks after the off-site meeting. This provides for the continuation of the process, the review of action steps, and the planning of further development.

Because work families are devised to increase production, they need to address very specific questions. The following checklist is useful:

Effective Work Methods

Do all members clearly understand the role of the team?
Are time scales explicit?
Does everyone have distinct tasks?
Are there crystal-clear targets to aim for?

Are the tasks and people well organized?

Are members aware of the commercial context of their objectives?

Have individual targets been clearly set?

Is performance being properly monitored?

Are there careful and regular reviews of progress?

Is there a detailed action plan, with benchmarks included?

Strong Leadership and Control

Has the team been carefully briefed?

Does the leader demonstrate skills in creating a productive work family?

Is there a clearly defined hierarchy?

Is leadership allowed to change as the task changes?

Blend of Skills

Are the available resources adequate?

Have team members been trained in working together?

Are team members able to perform the necessary tasks?

Do team members have complementary personality characteristics?

Are steps taken to get the best out of all members?

Positive Climate

Are time scales realistic?

Is everyone totally committed?

Does everyone want to work together?

Is there total involvement?

Does the team have a wish to achieve?

Does the team believe in its capability?

Is there empathy, rather than sympathy?

Productive work families are a natural way to organize. Although there are important differences, the analogy between families and teams is sufficiently close to be meaningful. Managers are advised to think about their organizations as work families and to build teams to sustain high performance.

SUMMARY: CORE PRINCIPLES — PULLING TOGETHER

- Families are the building blocks of society.
- People need to relate closely to others.
- Teams are a source of energy and commitment.
- Teams are relevant at every level of organization.
- Teams must be taught to avoid Groupthink.
- Teams should be carefully constructed.
- Teams should understand and practice team building.
- Team consultants should work with an established methodology.
- Team leaders are responsible for developing their own teams.

FIVE PRACTICAL STEPS TO ENCOURAGE THE PULLING-TOGETHER VALUE

1. Invite two or three experienced team consultants to develop proposals for your top team building. Consider all suggestions and choose those that appear most valuable. Then undertake a team-building exercise and review its value.

2. Look at your current procedures for selecting members of new teams. Use the Belbin analysis as described previously (page 138) to help in assembling a full blend of personalities.

3. Get your own team together for a two-hour meeting. Use a flip chart to list the answers to these three questions:

   ● What things do we do well now as a team?
   ● What should we be aiming to achieve in the future?
   ● What actions should be taken and by whom to improve team performance?

   At the end of the session, review whether the exercise has proved successful. If the answer is yes, then repeat it each month.

4. Close relationships are a necessary ingredient of effective teamwork. Select team members who will work well together and invite them to experiment by attending an "outward bound" type experience for three to four days. Wait three months and then review the results. Continue with the experiment if the results are promising.

5. Bring a video system into your next team meeting (with the prior agreement of all concerned) and record an hour of typical discussion. Replay the tape, stopping periodically for analysis, and produce a checklist of ideas for improvement. Implement the ideas and bring back the video recorder in three months' time to assess improvement.

REFERENCES

1. Tolstoy, L. (1954). *Anna Karenina*. London: Penguin Books.
2. Marx, K. (1975). *Selected Works*. USSR: Progress Publishers.
3. Trist, E. L. and Bamforth, K. W. (1951). Some Social and Psychological Consequences of the Long-Wall Method of Coal Getting. *Human Relations*, 3–38.

4. Walters, P. (1983, December 29). *Daily Telegraph*, p. 12.
5. Op. cit.
6. *Guidelines for Directors*. (1982). London: Institute of Directors.
7. Woodcock, M. (1989). *Team Development Manual*, 2nd ed. Aldershot, Surrey, U.K.: Gower; and Francis, D. and Young, D. (1979). *Improving Work Groups*. San Diego, CA: University Associates.
8. Belbin, M. (1981). *Management Teams: Why They Succeed or Fail*. Halstead, NY: Heinneman.

Law and Order: Justice Must Prevail

Every community develops a framework of laws that regulate conduct. These provide the ground rules of acceptable behavior. An organization exercises considerable power over the lives of its employees and their families, with managers operating as judge and jury, often without a right of appeal. The successful organization devises and honorably administers an appropriate system of rules and regulations. It adopts this value: *Justice must prevail.*

Organizations, like all other communities, establish rules of conduct which become codified into systems of laws. Most people recognize the fundamental importance of law in maintaining orderly and productive communities.

Just as managers act like the government of the country when they develop frameworks for administering justice, in effect, the organization is a microcosm of society. Management is, therefore, "micropolitics in action" and, in the exercise of power, managers become lawmakers, judges, and jury.

Managers regularize conduct and dispense justice for two reasons: first, because they are subject to national (or international) legal requirements, and second, because they must make "laws" themselves (codes of conduct, rules and regulations, procedures, etc.) to control and coordinate their organizations.

In this chapter we concentrate on the second aspect: the manager as lawmaker, judge, and jury. Of course, managers should comply both in letter and in spirit (although not always joyfully) with the law of the land. Managers tend to see interference by politicians as unhelpful. Much of the behavior in the workplace is regulated by national laws which can limit initiative and add to costs. Employers are no longer free to send children up chimneys or down coal mines! And quite right too.

TYPES OF ORGANIZATIONS

How much discipline, law, and order is desirable within an organization? While some managements maintain rigid discipline, other companies that are highly successful allow a relatively undisciplined environment in which to flourish. The contribution of law and order to organizations can be grasped only when we understand that some enterprises are inherently different in character from others. The essence of effective management is to choose an approach to law making that provides the correct balance between central regulation and individual initiative.

A simple analysis helps to answer the question. Begin by looking at the work done. Organizations do tasks that are either simple or difficult, routine or innovative. There are four possible permutations:

1	*2*	*3*	*4*
Organizations which perform simple and routine tasks	Organizations which perform difficult and routine tasks	Organizations which perform simple and innovative tasks	Organizations which perform difficult and innovative tasks

Four distinctly different types of organizations are needed to succeed at each permutation of tasks. The role of manager as lawmaker varies in each case. To demonstrate this point, we will examine each organizational type.

For Simple and Routine Tasks, a "Production" Organization is Required

Simple and routine tasks are typical of production or clerical organizations. Work has to be completed quickly and efficiently. People serve the system, and strong discipline is essential. Examples of this type of organization include postal delivery services, hand assembly plants, food-processing factories, and warehouse operations. Management can predict almost exactly what will happen, and they establish detailed codes of behavior to try and ensure that things go exactly as planned. Employees who are asked to conform to extensive rules and regulations, often develop cunning strategies for evading them. In the production organization, managers will prescribe as much behavior as possible, yet strive to avoid red-tape and meaningless regulations. The challenge for the organizational lawmaker in the production organization is to control fully what goes on without being labeled as a tyrant.

For Difficult and Routine Tasks, a "Professional" Organization is Required

Difficult but routine tasks are typical of craft or professional organizations. The work demands specialized knowledge and skill with professional workers making important decisions. In some ways, the organization should be the servant of its specialists. Examples of this type of organization include hospitals and universities. Managers cannot fully legislate for the behavior of specialists because too many complex circumstances occur. Discretion, therefore, passes to the craftsperson or professional worker. In professional organizations managers lay down guidelines for the selection of staff, set minimum standards of performance, and insist on professional development, regular training, and coordination. However, detailed or petty regulations will invoke little response; persuasion is an essential tool. The challenge to the organizational lawmaker in this form of organization is to set a common direction and achieve high standards while allowing individuals to cherish, develop, and protect their independence.

For Simple and Innovative Tasks, a "Decentralized" Organization is Required

Simple but innovative tasks are typical of decentralized organizations which need constantly to adjust to new situations in their volatile markets. Consider a business conglomerate, which may have businesses in aerospace, property, shipping, and insurance. Top management cannot understand each market and must establish management teams to run each type of business. Initiative and adaptability at the business team level are essential.

The principle is for each division to plan its own strategy. Because top managers cannot predict the specific requirements of each situation, they must develop the sensitivity of those in the front line. Teams must be created that can become adept at coping with specialized market conditions. Head office managers, who should be clear about objectives and standards, must realize that they cannot control all eventualities. They need to control by setting standards and by using training and feedback on performance, which are the appropriate techniques for regulating behavior. The challenge to the organizational lawmaker in this form of organization is to establish standards by which performance is judged and to enforce these while recognizing that high performance depends on individual workers taking initiative.

For Difficult and Innovative Tasks, an "Organic" Organization is Required

Difficult and innovative tasks are typical of research, development and other highly creative functions. New solutions must be found for state-of-the-art problems, and unconventional thinking is often required for a breakthrough. Work is flexible, often done in teams but sometimes alone. Examples of this kind of organization are advertising agencies, research laboratories, and some hi-tech production units. Management specifies problems to be solved but finds that it cannot set detailed objectives because too little is known about what is possible. Difficult choices, often based on technical debate, must be made, and managers take the roles of arbitrators and resource allocators. Unconventional behavior may be accepted from accomplished individuals. Very successful innovative companies have found that they have to fight against bureaucratic tendencies because these qualities inhibit creativity. Managers in organic organizations insist that regular reporting takes place and that a sense of urgency is maintained. However, they avoid rigid systems. The challenge for the organizational lawmaker in this form of organization is to regulate in extremely complex and ever-changing situations so that resources are well spent and time is not wasted through the pursuit of self-interest or indecision.

Each of these four organizational types presents particular management challenges. However, each form of organization has unique strengths and is the best choice for certain tasks. Managers should attune their lawmaking style to the needs of the situation. A comprehensive code of discipline is entirely suitable for a production organization but ludicrously irrelevant to the organic organization. The laws of the organization should of course be used to contribute to effectiveness, not to increase irrelevant bureaucracy.

THE TRUTH, THE WHOLE TRUTH, AND NOTHING BUT THE TRUTH

Many managers realize that enterprises thrive best when employees frankly disclose what they think and feel. Without openness, facts are hidden, and unhealthy organizational conflicts develop. *Openness*, which includes respect for individual opinions and support for the interests of minorities, can be defined as "clearly conveying facts, arguments, and perceptions to those who have influence." This definition of openness includes the following:

- Facts (descriptions of what is happening)
- Arguments (rational thinking and debate)
- Perceptions (emotional values and reactions)
- Influence (being heard by people who matter)

All these four elements are linked. Facts bring objectivity, thinking enables arguments to be rational, emotion gives passion, commitment and influence bring potency.

Why should managers deliberately encourage openness? The fundamental reason is that openness is an essential check on the potential abuse of power, especially managerial power. It is apparent that few large organizations are true democracies. Those individuals acquiring positions of organizational power are nominees of the existing establishment rather than freely elected representatives of the majority of employees. This situation makes organizations vulnerable to despotism. Checks and balances are required.

Managers should encourage openness for four reasons: to enhance the quality of decision making, to incorporate minority opinions, to sharpen the conscience of the organization, and to allow frustrations to be vented. We will examine each reason separately.

We need to enlarge on the research of Professor Irving Janus, which was summarized in Chapter 7. Janus alerted managers to the value of openness and to the inherent dangers of decision making without full expression of views. He vividly described a management ailment called *groupthink*.

Janus studied great blunders in decision making and found that top groups often become closed-minded and lose touch with reality. They see the world through their own rose-colored glasses and resist all attempts to change. He gave an insightful analysis of fiascos in the Cuban Bay of Pigs incident, the North Korean war, Pearl Harbor, the Vietnam War, and the Cuban missile crisis, and then evolved the following hypothesis: "The central theme of my analysis can be summarized in the generalization which I offer in the spirit of Parkinson's law: The more amiability and esprit de corps among the members of a policy making in-group, the greater is the danger that independent critical thinking will be replaced by groupthink, which is likely to result in irrational and dehumanizing actions directed against out groups."[1]

Janus suggests the deliberate encouragement of openness as an antidote to groupthink. He advocates, for example, that "one or more outside experts or qualified colleagues within the organization who are not core members should be invited to each meeting on a staggered basis and should be encouraged to challenge the views of the core members."[2]

You will recall that closed groups suffering from groupthink formulate their own interpretation of reality. They do not survey all of the available options; they discard options before examining them for non-obvious gains; they ignore expertise because of the bias of powerful group members; and they give insufficient consideration to the likely reactions of outside groups.

Since most management teams are close and cohesive decision-making groups, they are vulnerable to committing such blunders. All too often they develop an isolated approach and become a law unto themselves.

The best antidote to groupthink is openness, which requires evaluating views and proposals after comprehensive debate. Different perspectives, when voiced, shake and test illogical or unrealistic arguments. The quality of decision making largely depends on challenge and debate. Senior groups must make the decision and accept the consequences, but they reduce the risk of wrong judgment by seeking diverse viewpoints as part of their information-collection process. Insecure and blinkered managers fear to solicit views and take council, and they lose the capability to take wise decisions because of their narrow-mindedness: they readily become victims of groupthink.

WHO MAKES THE LAWS?

Many organizations have the complication of two lawmaking bodies in their midst. In addition to the formal management structure there is an alternative trade union system which also makes rules and has ways of achieving compliance. When these two power groups clash, as they often do, enormous effort is needed to seek common ground. Because almost all managers are committed to management-led organizations, they therefore see strong alternative power groups as a threat. The solution is easy to advise but difficult to practice: the management should maintain its power by demonstrating its supremacy through skills, competence, and principled good practice.

This requires the adoption of an approach to lawmaking appropriate to local needs. A management style effective in Mansfield, England, may become ridiculously ineffective when applied in Bombay or San Diego. To some extent, regional differences are observed within a country. In Britain, for example, a factory in Plymouth may have a very different character from one manufacturing similar products in Liverpool. Informal conventions shape behavior, like a giant, invisible puppeteer pulling strings in the organization to give it a distinctive character.

The study of the manager as lawmaker requires exploration of a further dimension: culture. Because organizational culture influences individuals, managers are advised to build a culture which facilitates high performance. When opportunities to mold culture occur, they are worth seizing. Although the task of the organization is more important than culture in determining the kinds of laws needed, culture influences how laws are applied and how justice is dispensed.

We have argued that managers should create relevant frameworks of law and order in organizations by first looking at the tasks undertaken. Managers are advised to study carefully their actual situation and devise appropriate strategies. The twelve questions that follow can assist in directing attention to those areas important for the organizational lawmaker:

1. What size is the organization?
2. What work is done?
3. How difficult are the tasks?
4. How much innovation is required?
5. What regulations should continue unchanged?
6. What regulations are decreasing performance and should be reduced or eliminated?
7. What new disciplines are likely to add to effectiveness?
8. How does the local community culture influence behavior?
9. How effectively could new regulations be enforced?
10. What historical factors limit freedom of action?
11. How strong are pressure groups which can resist management policy?
12. What are the key success factors of your industry?

CODES OF CONDUCT

At the most basic level, managers devise legal systems which regulate behavior in these areas:

- Attendance (hours, punctuality, etc.)

- Honesty (theft, sabotage, etc.)
- Conflict (physical violence, etc.)
- Discipline (who's in charge of what)
- Health and safety (legal and organizational requirements)
- Basic standards (hygiene, etc.)
- Commercial secrecy (what not to tell whom)
- Procedures for administering justice (including the involvement of appropriate trade unions, etc.)
- Punishments (type and appeal procedure)
- Rewards (remuneration, promotion, perks)

Organizations need legal systems to spell out and to enforce minimum codes of behavior. Such prescriptions should be just, clear, relevant, and, most important, enforceable. When unfair, obsolete, or unenforceable regulations exist, the integrity of the whole system is undermined.

Managers also act in the role of judge. In fact, they often combine the roles of lawmaker, judge, and jury even though, in almost all communities, particularly democratic ones, it has been decided that the legislature and the judiciary should be separate. Most national legal systems split even the two roles of the judge: that of determining guilt and that of passing sentence. However, many managers play all three of these roles.

Some would argue that management's power to act as lawmaker, judge, and jury is inherently unfair toward those who are managed. It certainly places a great responsibility on managers, who must strive hard to administer justice fairly. There are not many checks and balances built in to the legal systems of many organizations. To complicate further, the word *justice* describes a moving target—it changes with the times. Justice requires fair administration of prevailing laws.

It is useful to consider what *fairness* means. Of necessity, it must mean "in accord with a sense of natural justice." Schoolchildren talking of respected teachers describe them as firm but fair. Fairness is a quality that is much admired when present; the absence of fairness is despised. Managers increase the chances of fair judgment by adopting these five principles:

1. Selecting carefully those who will act as judges
2. Placing emphasis on collecting objective evidence
3. Maintaining clear and explicit procedures
4. Providing the opportunity for an accused person to state fully his or her case
5. Ensuring that there is a right of appeal

Rewards change behavior, and learning is reinforced by repetition. Conversely, behavior that is unrewarded tends to be reduced or eliminated. "Behavior modification" has proved to be a valid theory with animals as well as humans. For example, in one case, experimenters were able, by using suitable rewards, to cause a mouse to blush in only one ear. When regulations or laws in human communities are examined, the following insights emerge:

1. Appropriate behavior should be rewarded.
2. Repetition is usually necessary.
3. Feedback must happen quickly.
4. Inappropriate behavior must not be rewarded.
5. Punishment may aid unlearning.

This information is useful to managers because it emphasizes the positive use of systems of justice. Punishment is available, but only as a last resort. Most of the effort should be devoted to finding rapid ways of rewarding positive behavior. An organizational legal framework based on these principles will achieve positive motivation. Managements should not regulate by suppression and coercion. The acceptance of regulation and order is based on people recognizing the benefits of an organized life.

The cost of breaches in the rule of the law can be severe. If employees in a food factory are informally permitted to wear their hair uncovered, a woman might be severely injured when her long hair is caught in machinery. Because a director uses company funds for currency speculation, millions are lost. If poor time-keeping and sloppy standards are tolerated in a vehicle assembly plant with production efficiencies below that of similar plants on the continent, the factory will eventually close. No one gains and the derisory remarks about petty regulations sound hollow when "the chickens come home to roost."

Recently, we have seen many organizations rediscover the importance of regulations, partly inspired by American and Japanese management techniques. A good illustration is the fast-food business. For many years down-at-the-heel fast-food outlets were preeminent; then came McDonald's! The success of the McDonald's formula was like a cold shower to the opposition. McDonald's consistently maintained high standards and attracted more and more customers. There were two secrets: first, their business concept was sound, and second, McDonald's is highly structured and disciplined, a well-regulated example of the production organization described earlier in this chapter. Competitors, if they were to survive, had to revise their company approach to law and order and set new standards of performance and customer care.

The lessons of this chapter are fundamental. Successful organizations are open, fair, and orderly societies with appropriate legal systems. Managers must use their judicial powers wisely and constructively.

SUMMARY: CORE PRINCIPLES — JUSTICE MUST PREVAIL

- All organizations need legal systems.
- Managers must make laws and administer justice.
- Managers should work within the law of the land, but seek to influence national lawmakers to enact helpful legislation.
- Organizational laws should be fit for their purposes.

- "Production" organizations need to be very carefully controlled.
- "Professional" organizations need to maintain high standards of selection and training.
- "Decentralized" organizations need to be allowed to go their own way if the results are adequate.
- "Organic" organizations need to fight bureaucracy and encourage teamwork.
- Managers should review the special character of their own organization prior to making laws.
- Corporate legal systems should lay down basic codes of conduct.
- Managers should be aware that they act as judge and jury, and that few checks and balances exist in most organizations to ensure that justice is done.
- Organizational laws are best used to provide positive motivation.

FIVE PRACTICAL STEPS TO ENSURE THE JUSTICE-MUST-PREVAIL VALUE

1. Ask each manager to do the following:
   (a) List those regulations which are kept.
   (b) List those regulations which are ignored.
   (c) List those regulations which appear irrelevant.
   (d) List any new regulations considered desirable.
   Use the information to produce a detailed report for the top management team, as a prelude to a review of regulations in your organization.
   Invite a practicing lawyer specializing in industrial law to visit you and do the following:
   (a) Assess how far your present practices conform to legal requirements.

     (b) Comment on justice in your organization, in particular how your approach would stand up if it were "on trial."

2. Arrange for an organizational consultant or researcher to conduct a one-day seminar for top management on how organizations control and regulate themselves. Try to obtain an insight into how organizations vary according to tasks performed (contingency theory). Use the information to analyze your own organization and determine whether your internal legal system should be altered in principle or application.

3. Examine your present internal regulations and codes of conduct to determine whether they are expressed positively or negatively. Use the skills of your marketing department to devise a revised guide which is comprehensive, comprehensible, and positive.

4. Look afresh at procedures for dispensing discipline to try to achieve quicker feedback so that the punishment follows soon after the crime. Develop criteria for judging success, and devise a means of monitoring performance.

REFERENCES

1. Janus, I. L. (1972). *Victims of Groupthink*. London: Harcourt Brace Jovanovich, p. 130.
2. Ibid, p. 214.

Managing the Environment

CHAPTER 13

Defense: Know Thine Enemy

For many organizations it is a dog-eat-dog world. In every commercial organization, there are talented people planning strategies to increase their business at the expense of the competition. Many noncommercial organizations find themselves under threat from those who provide their funds. The successful organization studies external threats and formulates a strong defense. It adopts this value: *Know thine enemy.*

Every living organism can be threatened, and organizations are no exception. There are enemies without and within. Because the world is a dangerous place, it is imperative to study anything that might be a threat.

In this chapter we consider these three questions:

Why take a warlike approach to management?
Who are the enemies outside the organization?
Who are the enemies within the organization?

WHY TAKE A WARLIKE APPROACH TO MANAGEMENT?

It is easy to underestimate the importance of military thinking to strategic planning. Consider this example: One of the reasons for the success of Japanese business in the postwar period has been identified as the "Samurai" factor.[1]

The time-honored samurai principles are the following:

- Know the opposition.
- Live harmoniously.
- Master all weapons.
- Concentrate your resources.
- Respect uncertainty.
- If you cannot win, form an alliance.
- Fight at a time of your own choosing.
- Seize and retain the initiative.
- Balance strategy with detail.

Many Japanese leaders, who owe much to the Samurai tradition, perceive their activities as a benign form of warfare. In order to understand how such warlike values provide a competitive edge, it is necessary to examine the principles of good generalship.

A classic analysis made by General Von Clausewitz[2] identified the nine principles of successful warfare:

Principle One: Every operation should be directed towards a clearly defined, decisive, and attainable objective.

Although this principle reads like an obvious or "motherhood" statement, there are many cases in which it has been ignored. Another military historian, Colonel Summers,[3] describes the results of a research study which showed that "almost 70% of the Army Generals who managed the [Vietnam] war were uncertain as to its objective. [This demonstrated] a deep-seated strategic failure: the inability of policy makers to frame tangible, obtainable goals."

There are many cases in which nonmilitary organizations have suffered the same fate: Jaguar cars in the 1970s and Midland Bank's takeover of the Crocker Bank are two examples.

Principle Two: Seize, retain, and exploit the initiative.

A strong defense will deter and protect, but it will not win a war. An offensive initiative is needed, although a direct frontal assault rarely leads to victory.

There are five ways to seize the initiative:

1. **Frontal attack:** an assault against the enemy's main source of strength
2. **Flank attack:** an attempt to bypass the main lines of defense
3. **Guerrilla attack:** an assault from behind
4. **Penetration:** an attack from within
5. **Self-attack:** an attack against your own capability in order to confront your weaknesses and bring about self-improvement

Principle Three: Concentrate combat power at the decisive place and time.

Always there are some decisive moments when one side gains long-term advantage. An aim of strategic thinking is to see the potential of a decisive victory before it occurs and amass forces to win that battle.

There are many cases in which organizations have been overwhelmed by the size, ferocity, or skill of the opposition. The chief skill needed by the management is to deploy your resources at the point of your competitor's weakness, an example of the art of positioning.

Principle Four: Allocate minimum combat power to the secondary efforts.

Since it is impossible to be strong everywhere, it is necessary to deploy forces in sufficient concentrations to make a decisive difference. This principle is often ignored by growing businesses which take on too much and spread themselves too thinly. Overambition is a common fault. Hence weakness and inadequate resources are devoted to the primary objectives. Even large companies can become overextended. For example, the Japanese earth-moving equipment company, Komatsu, was very successful until it tried to defeat Caterpillar on its own ground in the United States. It is vital to determine the scope of operations and not to become overextended.

Principle Five: Place the enemy at a position of disadvantage through the flexible use of your combat power.

Once a strategy becomes static, it provides opponents with the time to prepare their attack. Constant change gives you an edge, since it takes time for the enemy to detect what you are doing.

This factor means that organizations must get used to constantly reorganizing and developing new ways of addressing old problems. Creativity is always required. An organization needs to determine its competitive edge (whether it is price, quality, or service) and work at maintaining a real advantage.

Principle Six: For every objective there should be a unity of command under one responsible commander.

Confusion about who is in charge has led to many blunders, both military and commercial. There is no doubt that one of the most effective ways to coordinate efforts is to make one person responsible; the integration then takes place in one person's brain.

Principle Six draws attention to the need for a "responsible" commander. The centralization of decision-making authority in one person has inherent risks. It is vital that such people should be capable.

This principle also causes us to question the use of matrix and consensus-management techniques, as these spread responsibility and can create confusion and evasion.

Principle Seven: Never permit the enemy to acquire an unexpected advantage.

It is imperative to constantly assess your competition and predict all of the hostile actions that they might be capable of undertaking. The story of the Trojan Horse has been repeated in many contexts since 1184 B.C.

It is essential to have an intimate knowledge of your industry, and of the competitive environment. Early warning signs of an enemy offensive can often be detected, despite your opponent's best efforts to disguise their intent. All too often the challenges of the moment cause managers to wear blinkers and ignore the threats until it is too late.

Principle Eight: Strike the enemy at a time, place, and in a manner for which the enemy is unprepared.

It is difficult to surprise opponents at the strategic level, but often tactical advantage can be gained. This requires a conscious effort to keep the opposition unsure of your true objectives. By spreading confusion, you gain more opportunity to create surprise.

Speed is also needed. Rapid change is, in essence, confusing to those who are not party to your plan. The faster you move, the more likely it is that you can strike unexpectedly.

Principle Nine: Keep all plans simple, because even the simplest of plans is difficult to execute.

A simple plan is needed because many people must take initiatives to turn the plan into a reality. Because complex plans are difficult to interpret, people make invalid interpretations and effort is dissipated. Plans have to be implemented in less than ideal circumstances. Sustaining effort is always a problem. Simple plans enable individual efforts to be focused and supervision exercised.

WHO ARE THE ENEMIES OUTSIDE THE ORGANIZATION?

All organizations have potential competitors. A competitor is "an organization that is perceived by customers as providing an equivalent good/service to your organization and which meets a similar need or want."

In order to study the competition, it is necessary to organize an intelligence operation. This requires the following:

- A "war room" which is where all competitor information is stored and displayed
- A task force which contains senior line managers, an excellent business analyst, and some foot soldiers
- Speed, to prevent the intelligence task force from becoming bureaucratic
- Strict standards of objectivity
- A list of your actual competitors today
- A list of potential competitors
- A file of each competitor which contains
  - Their annual reports and accounts for the last few years
  - Relevant press cuttings on the competitor's company
  - Any specialized consultancy studies available
  - Details of patents and potential new patents
- A file on your industry which contains
  - Statistics on the market and its growth (historical and projected)
  - Specialized written assessments of the market

- A list of the "bad" competitors (i.e., those who could and might seriously damage your business), with a detailed file on each
- A detailed history of each competitor, including points of the history of each
- An assessment of the dangers of your being technologically leapfrogged
- A study of each "bad" competitor's management team:
  - Who has the power?
  - What is his/her history?
  - What are the top team strengths and weaknesses?

It is vital to involve the top team in ensuring that the research data is relevant. Brief reports for the top team (intelligence briefings) should be prepared. The key data should be presented in easy-to-visualize charts, tables, graphs, cartoons, etc. The process should be repeated often.

Not all threats are negative. Even though fair competition is a form of attack, this external challenge, when ethical, is a force which sharpens and stimulates.

WHO ARE THE ENEMIES WITHIN THE ORGANIZATION?

Internal threats are usually destructive, because they undermine the integrity of the organization. Like woodworm in the timbers of an old building, organizational civil war often produces catastrophic results.

There are seven potential threats to the internal integrity of organizations. These are as follows:

1. Lack of focus so that the organization loses its way
2. Inadequate management development so that resources are wasted (see Chapter 5)

3. Poor integration between functions so that coordination is weak (see Chapter 8) and low commercial awareness so that survival is threatened (see Chapter 9)
4. Slow innovation so that the organization becomes obsolete (see Chapter 14)
5. Lack of consensus so that the objectives of the organization are not shared by all employees and people do not care about the success of the organization (see Chapters 10 and 11)
6. Structured attacks from alternative power groups so that management's freedom is confined

We shall examine the first and the last of these threats (the others have been discussed in earlier chapters):

Issue One: Lack of focus so that the organization loses its way.

Lack of focus is a familiar managerial problem. In our consulting practice, we are often asked to help top management teams in their search for a clear and viable identity. We find that it is vital for each strategically distinct unit to identify its "Strategic Driving Force."[4] There are twelve possibilities:

Strategic Driving Force One: State-of-the-Art Capability

This organization is devoted to being a leader in its chosen field. The "state-of-the-art" organization generates business by doing things in more advanced or more clever ways than anyone else does. The organization is a powerhouse of creativity and is constantly changing as new technology develops. Customers are attracted by getting the best or newest goods or services.

Strategic Driving Force Two: Professional Service

This organization is devoted to providing its customers with highly skilled individual services. The professional service organization enables qualified individuals to carry out their specialized tasks. Customers are attracted to professional service organizations because they have complex human needs which such an organization can meet.

Strategic Driving Force Three: Product Producer

This organization is devoted to producing goods or services and offering them to defined markets. Product-producer organizations have product ranges which are not tailor-made for individual customers. Customers are attracted by products which are desirable and good value for the money.

Strategic Driving Force Four: Experience Provider

This organization is devoted to providing people with experiences which they enjoy or value. The experience-provider organization generates business by meeting a human need for sensation, stimulation, or edification. The experience provider organization aims to understand totally and fulfill a need or want. This may be for entertainment (as in a theater), excitement (as on an action holiday), fantasy (as in a strip club), interest (as in a museum), or spiritual experience (as in a church). Such organizations concentrate on the depth and breadth of the receiver's experience.

Strategic Driving Force Five: Market Server

This organization is devoted to fulfilling all the needs of a defined market. There are many markets and market segments like fishermen, electrical contractors, stamp collectors, secretaries, and so on. Customers are attracted to the market-server organization because it can meet most or all of their needs.

Strategic Driving Force Six: System Provider

This organization is devoted to enabling other organizations to communicate or coordinate. The system-provider organization generates business by enabling complex operations to be performed. Such systems may be electronic, logistical, or managerial; the essence is providing a capability to others which enables them to manage complexity.

Strategic Driving Force Seven: Production Contractor

This organization is devoted to providing a facility for others to get things built, constructed, repaired, adapted, or manufactured. The production-contractor organization generates business by enabling specialized tasks to be done for those without the ability or resources to do the work themselves. The essence of their business is that they contract to supply specific services which maintain or add value to products.

Strategic Driving Force Eight: Profit Cow

This organization is devoted to making money for its owners. It is solely a resource for making a profit and is exploited only so long as it is the best way of using the capital tied up in ownership. All managerial decisions are made with the intention of maximizing profitability. The profit-cow organization generates business by providing channels to exploit the commercial acumen of its owners.

Strategic Driving Force Nine: Resource Ownership

This organization is devoted to acquiring valuable resources and exploiting them. There are two types of resource ownership enterprises. The first owns land, space, minerals, raw materials, crops, animals, or things cultivated and grown. This type of resource-ownership organization generates business because it possesses and distributes commodities which others need and want. The second type of resource ownership is the large conglomerate which acquires a portfolio of companies that are measured on their performance. The portfolio is treated as an "estate" and adapted to maximize profitability over the medium and long term.

Strategic Driving Force Ten: Distribution Capability

This organization is devoted to moving physical products to wherever they are needed, by air, rail, sea, road, canal, space flight, and so on. The distribution-capability organization generates business by providing systems and vehicles for efficient transportation of tangible items without damaging them. It exploits its distribution capability in as many ways as possible.

Strategic Driving Force Eleven: Maintenance of Order

This organization is devoted to maintaining order. It protects people, property, services, peace, and the rights of citizens. The maintenance-of-order organization generates business by enabling other activities to proceed unhindered. There are two types of maintenance-of-order organizations. The first is concerned with security. On the national scale, the armed forces have this role, whereas at the community level, local police, courts, security guards, and so on perform similar functions. The second type of maintenance-of-order organization provides services like cleaning, repairing, painting, maintaining, monitoring, inspecting, and surveying.

Strategic Driving Force Twelve: Self-Expression

This organization is devoted to providing facilities for members to do what they need or want to do. Satisfaction includes enjoyment, self-expression, enlightenment, comradeship, support, and stimulation. The self-expression organization sustains itself because people wish to contribute and give voluntarily. Such organizations are frequently noncommercial.

These twelve strategic driving forces provide the basis to choose a viable compelling vision which becomes the single driving force of an organization. Because the viability of the choice is partly determined by the environment, the analysis of enemies is vital. Once determined, *all* aspects of the organization should be shaped to actualize the driving force.

> *Issue Seven:* Structured attacks from alternative power groups so that management's freedom is confined.

The seventh threat, which has been particularly important in recent years, largely concerns the role of trade unions. These institutions have repeatedly demonstrated that they can undermine the managerial power base. The picture, however, is patchy; some managers have struck constructive bargains with trade unions, and others admit a grudging respect for their single-mindedness. The extent to which managers are affected by trade union activities varies greatly.

The stance of trade unions should not be taken lightly. There is no doubt that many trade unions have a distinguished record. An examination of their history over the past century will reveal that many honorable battles have been fought against managerial injustice.

In the past exploitation was practiced by bosses. The image of young children working down coal mines is sufficient to make the point. Organized protest proved the only effective way to counter such abuses. The fact that trade unions developed in every industrial country demonstrates the universality of the need for them.

In many countries trade unions have gained strength by differentiating themselves from employers: as such they may be accused of promoting—sometimes explicitly, sometimes insidiously—class warfare. They require periodic conflict to give them a sustained raison d'être. So trade unions sometimes seek opportunities to contest management and often perceive themselves as "winning battles." The interdependence of so much of industry gives unions enormous power to disrupt.

Let us examine the threat in more detail. On the surface, trade unions appear to be fighting for the downtrodden. Ironically, though, their struggles have often had the opposite effect. Nobel prize-winning economist Friedrich Hayek, writing about the British economy, stated: "As long as the general opinion makes it politically impossible to deprive the Trades Unions of their coercive power, an economic recovery in Great Britain is also impossible. . . . It is an illusion that the problem Britain now faces can be solved by negotiation with the present Trades Union leaders. They own their power precisely to the scope for abusing the privileges which the law has granted them. It is the rank and file of the workers, including many Trades Union members who ultimately suffer from the abuse."[5]

Although the abuse of trade-union power has been the biggest potential inner threat over the past fifty years, there are many other hazards which erode management power. There has been a decline in the acceptance of the legitimacy of authority in society. In the U.K., changing attitudes towards the police, urban riots, and sports-ground hooliganism are all symptoms of this.

A management's power base requires a sense of unity. The only sound basis for any organization is a group of people pulling together for a common end. It is disastrous for an organization to lose sight of customers' needs and to waste energy in ponderous internal debate. The flabbiness which results from such internal struggles is costly to an organization's health.

On balance, attack is the best form of defense. If managers are humane and professional, they counter all of the seven threats listed at the beginning of this chapter. This is achievable only if managements take a responsible stance towards their work force.

For example, trade-union strength is partly a result of the inadequacy and unprofessionalism of management. An unprincipled organization deserves to be constantly harassed by threats, but a well-managed organization does not.

We have seen many companies win by changing their posture and redefining the conventional contract between the company and the work force. This provides a crucial foundation for an integrated organization. For example, the Nissan company made it clear that it would build a car plant in England only if it negotiated a satisfactory agreement with a single union, which eliminated demarcation and discouraged disruptive conflicts.

John Harvey-Jones, ex-chairman of ICI (Imperial Chemical Industries), puts it this way: "The reality of the future is that the interests of trades unions, union membership and management lie together and it is the responsibility of management to take the lead in making this collaboration more effective and more creative."[6]

Where the internal battles have been won, there are great benefits. The start-up of the new "sinter" steel-making plant at Redcar in northeast England was delayed in 1978 by the Boilermakers Union, which refused to operate with new manning levels and working practices. Yet with agreement, there is now full flexibility among the forty-strong workforce, down by twenty since commissioning. Operators have replaced tradesmen's mates on maintenance tasks. Craftsmen work across craft boundaries. Through excellent management, comprehensive training, and a cooperative work force, the plant holds the world's sinter output record. The plant operates at almost 100 percent efficiency, product quality is unrivaled, and energy use is at better than Japanese or European standards.[7]

There are some interesting initiatives in seeking common ground between employees and managers. One particularly valuable effort was put together by the Industrial Society, which produced a declaration from twelve industrialists and trade-union leaders. The principles, which make interesting reading, argue that the best form of defense is not to go to war in the first place.

The key points include these:

- Management should recognize employees' right to belong to an independent trade union, recognize a representative trade union for negotiating purposes, and encourage employees to belong to a trade union when it is recognized.
- Trade unions should recognize the responsibility of those in management to concern themselves with the interests of all employees; seek to resolve interunion disputes; reflect the views of their members; and seek to involve all of them through effective procedures.
- Management should consult the trade unions before deciding upon changes which affect their members, and should enable employees to participate in the formulation of relevant management policies.
- Trade unions should accept the challenge of proper consultation and share the responsibility for developing the correct policies for change, by making suggestions and using the knowledge of their members to make the operation successful.
- Management should be efficient, inventive, and ingenious in expanding the scope for real jobs.
- Trade unions should give commitment to the success of the enterprise and work for the creation of more jobs.

The Industrial Society's document argues that the proper relationship between management and other employees is a bargain based on an acceptance of the importance of commercial viability. We agree that the best form of defense is to make the thought of war impossible. Management must manage and resist potential threats to its power. This is an aggressive stance which, the authors believe, can be justified only when management does its job well and adopts high principles.

We began this chapter by looking at how to win battles. We will end by looking at the guidelines for protection. There are ten strategies for defense which have proved their worth since the Trojan War. The ingredients of successful defense are these:

- Awareness of threat so that we are always watchful
- A good system for gathering intelligence so that we know our enemy
- Constant training so that we are ready for the enemy
- Predicting the likely nature of an attack so that we can be ready
- Contingency planning so that we can swing into action without delay
- Using our imagination so that we can outwit the enemy
- Keeping our defensive equipment up-to-date so that we are not outgunned
- Engendering pride so that people feel that they have something for which to fight
- Giving emotional support to the troops so that their morale remains high
- Having high-quality generals so that people are well led

These rules of defense are directly applicable within organizations, but there is a danger. In adopting an aggressively defensive stance, the manager may well invoke the feared behavior. Belligerence for its own sake is counterproductive. However, there is no excuse for inaction; enemies must be identified and fought.

SUMMARY: CORE PRINCIPLES — KNOW THINE ENEMY

- Managers should be wary of threats.
- Clarity of objectives is essential.
- Strive to retain the initiative.
- Concentrate your resources.

- Retain flexibility and the capacity to surprise.
- Ensure that the command structure is 100 percent clear.
- Predict the threats from your potential enemies.
- Keep plans simple: do not confuse yourself.
- Fair competition is a positive threat (it sharpens you).
- Internal threats are usually destructive.
- Lack of focus is a major threat; the top team needs to determine the strategic driving force of the organization.
- Structured opposition, particularly from trade unions, has been a serious internal threat; management needs to reduce dissent and eliminate the reasons for trade union power.
- Finding common ground (as in the Industrial Society Declaration) is helpful.
- A strong defense is always needed.

FIVE PRACTICAL STEPS TO ENSURE THE KNOW-THINE-ENEMY VALUE

1. Arrange for a military historian to give a presentation to your top team. Ensure that the principles of military successes are well explained. Examine your strategy and tactics to see whether you are lacking. Try to find practical ways to implement the proven principles.

2. Consider the twelve strategic driving forces described in this chapter and choose the one that is right for your organization. Include the definition in your mission statement, and require all senior functional managers to report on how they are going to adapt their department's performance to assist in the enhancement of the chosen strategic driving force.

3. Create a top management study group to assess what benefits the organization and its employees gain from trade unions. Get to know the personal philosophies of

relevant trade-union officials and elected representatives. Try to determine the level of threat which each presents. Develop alternative means for people to express their opinions (e.g., attitude surveys) so that the power base of unions is weakened. Be sure they know that their opinions are heard. Act on the basis of your views about how industrial relations should be managed.

4. Ensure that your personnel professionals get the best possible training in negotiation skills. Ask them to visit those organizations with good records of defense against internal threats. Use intensive training to improve their skills.

5. List organizations that have achieved good relationships with their trade unions. Visit them to find out how they did it. See how many of the lessons can be employed in your own organization. Carefully review what benefits are gained by employees and seek to offer these by management initiative.

REFERENCES

1. See review of Joseph Rudzinski and Harutoshi Muyazami, "The Samurai Factor," in *The Work Research Unit Bulletin*, Spring 1987, p. 8, London.
2. Von Clausewitz, Gen. C. (1968). *On War*. London: Penguin Books.
3. Summers, Col. H. G. (1982). *On Strategy*. Novato, CA: Presidio Press.
4. See *Unblocking Organizational Communication* (op cit) for an extended discussion of this concept.
5. Hayek, F. (1980). *1980s Unemployment and the Unions*. London: Institute of Economic Affairs.
6. Harvey-Jones, J. (1984, May). *Personal Management*, p. 41.
7. *Lloyds Bank Review*, 152, pp. 21–22.

C H A P T E R 14

Competitiveness:
Survival of the Fittest

The capacity to be competitive is the only surefire recipe for survival. Usually this fact is recognized at the top level, but it is less likely that the message is understood throughout the rest of the organization. The successful organization takes all necessary steps to be competitive. It knows that in the world of commerce, it is the best who survive and the weakest who go to the wall. It adopts this value: *Survival of the fittest.*

In 1984 the Chinese Communist Party announced radical changes in their philosophy of industrial development. A thirty-nine-page document, which described a new structure for their industry, stated that productive organizations would be expected to make profits and pay taxes.[1] The State would "force businesses to compete so that only the best survive." These radical proposals, said to have been devised by China's elder statesman, Deng Xiaoping, were designed to redress the "lack of vitality" in industry. The document states that "enthusiasm, initiative, and creativity of the urban enterprises for production and operations, as well as eight million workers and staff members, must be brought into full play." One of the authors spent two weeks in China visiting many organizations. He saw a close parallel between Deng Xiaoping's reforms and some of the basic principles of nineteenth-century enterprise. Also he observed that China appears to have discovered the basic truth that competition encourages people to excel, and remarked that "many of the Chinese I met may call themselves communists, but to me they were rapidly becoming capitalists in overalls."

Human beings compete with each other in many situations. The "survival of the fittest" principle runs deep. Teenage boys in the African Kau tribe spend hours weaving their hair into fantastic designs in their eager quest to be considered the most handsome in the group. Greek athletes developed the Olympic Games to test physical prowess. The retired widows vie with each other to travel to the world's most interesting places. Everywhere competition brings out the latent potential in people. A runner uses the services of a pacer to push him through the first part of the race, then competes with the clock for the final impetus. Reluctant joggers know it is difficult to puff and pant around their course alone; it is easier to take exercise playing a close game of squash. Although human nature is extremely adaptable, competitiveness is such a pervasive force that, for practical purposes, it can be called a human "instinct."

Competition, which is a trigger for the release of human energy, can be purposefully used by managers in the pursuit of excellence. Managers should become more aware of the positive merits of competition. Essentially, competition is a way of organizing human affairs that clearly demonstrates who wins and provides a motivating factor that has led to outstanding achievement.

Competitiveness is frequently derided as a symptom of a juvenile mentality. For example, some schools prevent children from entering athletic competitions on the basis that competitions encourage elitism. Yet most people enjoy coming in contact with excellence. The film *Chariots of Fire* explored the depths of the competitive urge. In this film the athletes compete with other runners, their social environment, and, most powerfully, with themselves. The result is a beautiful and moving portrait of a superb human achievement that emerged through competition.

However, like all powerful tools, competition, when used in the wrong way, rapidly becomes counterproductive. Excessive competition provokes various groups that should be working together into becoming sworn enemies, and individuals into attempting to outdo each other instead of collaborating. Destructive competition must be identified and fought. The essence of using the energizing force of competition is to know who is your real opponent.

Winning is a learnable competence. Often people will admit that they lack assertion, drive, and a winner's mentality. This problem can be traced to a lack of development in personal competitiveness. It can be persuasively argued that over the past decades, advisers to management have placed too much emphasis on collaboration and harmonization and have tended, wrongly, to see consensus as the superior way of achieving the best.

A worthy opponent should be greatly valued. In London the story is told in Westminster about a new member of parliament who referred to the opposition parties as "the enemy." He was soon told by an experienced back bencher, "always remember, the opposition are your opponents, not your enemy. They sharpen your wits. Your enemies are on this side of the house because they are the people who would personally benefit from your downfall."

Competition can be a creative and motivating force in the work place, but, when it is the sole principle that guides behavior, it undermines the quality of life. Someone who relentlessly competes for the sole purpose of self-aggrandizement may gain material riches but is driven by obsession and often finds financial achievements hollow. Competition is an essential ingredient for a productive managerial philosophy but needs to be enriched by a desire to enhance the quality of life.

The British Institute of Directors[2] says: "The free enterprise system depends fundamentally on the ability of individuals to choose to spend their money on the products of one business rather than those of another. Nothing is more calculated to bring free enterprise into disrepute than attempts to secure an unfair advantage over customers, whether by failure to disclose information relevant to the customer's choice, by attempts to set aside statutory safeguards for customers, or by an unwillingness to take adequate account of, or provide adequate compensation for, possible damages to health implicit in a particular product. The customer is the businessman's friend, not his enemy."

COMPETITION IN ORGANIZATIONS

Within an organization, competition should be focused to raise standards, maintain a high level of achievement, and motivate. We will examine competition at these five levels:

1. Individual versus individual
2. Team versus team
3. Unit versus unit
4. Organization versus organization
5. International competition

The competitive principle is a double-edged sword. When used unwisely, it results in waste, backbiting, secrecy, and interpersonal sniping. Organizational performance decreases when those who should cooperate adopt a competitive stance. This does not mean that the principle of competition should be abandoned: rather, it must be used selectively and judiciously.

LEVEL ONE: INDIVIDUAL VERSUS INDIVIDUAL

Competition is first encountered in the process of recruiting new people. Because the quality of human resources is crucial to effectiveness, it is imperative that the best people are chosen. It is worth making great effort to facilitate genuine competition between job applications. Choice at the recruitment stage is one of management's most valued devices for maintaining control.

The individuality of each person should be recognized. Selection is common to all species. Charles Darwin studied the turtles of the Galápagos Islands to discover the principles of evolution,[3] but he could also have looked at successful organizations to find ample evidence to support his theories. The successful concept is simple: the fittest are the ones who thrive. The successful manager seeks to select those who are the "fittest."

Within an organization, competition between individuals can be a uniquely valuable motivator but must be carefully handled to prevent "losers" from giving up, becoming resentful, and failing to "play the game." Success should be something to which all can aspire, and continued successes are needed to sustain motivation.

The first focus of competition lies within the individual. This can be encouraged by the most enduring management technique, Management by Objectives, which has been in use for more than twenty-five years. The essential points of this technique are valuable; boss and subordinate agree on measurable targets, which become psychological contracts. Management by Objectives uses the basic form of the competitive principle; people are provided with the means to compete against agreed performance levels.

In some jobs it is possible to use competition between individuals as a primary motivating force. Many salespeople, after leaving their homes early in the morning, bounce into their potential customers' premises full of joviality and positiveness. They are partly motivated by relentless competition with other salesmen. Although a salesman might not want to be at the top of the tree, he has to compete simply to keep his job. One salesman said, "I spend my life being measured, and I know my place in the pecking order all the time. It's the thing that drives me on!"

LEVEL TWO: TEAM VERSUS TEAM

Competition can also operate within groups. Here the principle is to set collective standards for achievement. Next time you go into a McDonald's restaurant, look at the name badges of the staff. Some have stars, while others have blank spaces. Each star represents a tested level of competence in a particular aspect of the operation of the store. One star is gained for counter service, another for preparing french fries, and so on. Many employees will work hard to achieve the set standards because they are motivated by a visible reward. They are not competing against one another, but instead for a prize. In a marathon run, all finishers are usually presented with a medal. This medal demonstrates achievement, which means a lot to even the last finisher. The standard has been achieved.

For many workers the competitive principle may seem irrelevant. Because one job is interwoven with another, individual achievement is difficult to identify. However, it is often possible to use the second level of competition: the work team as the unit of comparison. Teams can often be encouraged to strive to demonstrate their superior potency and competence.

The following questions can help you to decide whether interteam competition is a relevant motivational technique for your organization.

- Do the teams have similar objectives?
- Can there be objective measures of performance?
- Are few areas of collaboration needed?
- Can rewards be given for success?
- Are all teams likely to react favorably to competition?
- Can feedback on relative success be given quickly?

If the answer to these questions is yes, then the teams are likely to benefit from interteam competition. This approach demands the following:

- A fair comparison
- Rapid exchange of performance data
- The chance for all teams either to win or to fail
- Prizes for success (recognition is often enough)
- Leadership that helps turn the experience of failure into a desire to win next time

UNIT VERSUS UNIT

Sometimes the third level of competition is useful: organizational units can compete with each other. Chains of retail stores often set comparative targets for shop performance which are regularly shared and prizes given to the successful. Some of the motivational techniques may seem juvenile. For example, one large electrical retailer rewards outstanding stores by a visit from a busload of wild-looking figures dressed in weird animal skins. These creatures enter the shop with much razzmatazz, cavort with the staff, and present prizes. Ridiculous? Of course it is, but because people enjoy it, it helps energize their working lives.

Large organizations are frequently structured into units or divisions, each devoted to a particular market. Direct competition is difficult because these units have unique problems and opportunities. However, progressive accountants can provide techniques for statistical comparison, such as the following:

- Capital employed
- Return on assets employed
- Gross profit
- Net profit
- Growth trends
- Market shares
- Output per employee
- Cost comparison with competitors
- Investment in research and development

- Level of complaints
- Added value per employee

Such comparative data, when carefully analyzed, enables apparently dissimilar units to be compared for competitive purposes and provides an essential basis for decision making and communication. Few accountants would volunteer that their most important task is to exploit the competitive urge, but we see this role as one of their most important contributions.

Successful organizations have found ways to institutionalize competition. One of the authors consults with a vigorous British electronics company which needs to innovate continuously in order to survive. Their technical-development program had been controlled by a complex procedure, but top management became aware that their rational planning system was filtering out rogue ideas and opportunistic chances. Therefore, they instituted a parallel system to encourage "product champions." A competition was held in which any individual could propose new product ideas. The company gave three months' "sabbatical" to allow the winning idea to be explored. At least one person in the company was on sabbatical at all times. The resultant flow of creativity was of great value.

LEVEL FOUR: YOUR ORGANIZATION VERSUS THE REST

The fourth level of competition is almost always desirable: competition between organizations. If one paper-bag manufacturer competes with another, both are sharpened and kept dynamic. Without competition, neither company has the strong incentive to change or critically reexamine existing practices.

Organizations must compete to meet the real needs of the customer. The former chairman of Unilever, Sir David Orr, said,

"I always want to keep a close eye on the customer. If the business is not continually adjusting to what the customer requires, then trouble is probably just around the corner."

There is always the risk that another organization will make your product or supply your service better or cheaper than you can. This threat should keep everyone on their toes, but there is an interesting side effect: organizations strive to be different from their competitors by finding and maintaining a "sustainable competitive advantage." In this way innovation is encouraged and creativity valued. Lord Murray, retired general secretary of the British Trades Union Congress, said, "Industry has to deliver the goods in the right quantity and of the right quality at the right time." It is ironic that the entrenched and protected viewpoints of many trade union leaders have done much in the past to prevent British organizations from achieving this goal.

Over the past two decades we have lived through an interesting experiment in abandoning the competitive principle; it is called the Common Agricultural Policy of the European Economic Community (EEC).* What was the result? Despite the endeavors of bureaucrats and "Eurocrats" (a popular term for bureaucrats working for the EEC), there has been massive overproduction of some agricultural products, a situation considered "totally lunatic" by many observers. This would never have happened if the free flow of competition had been permitted. Economic absurdities are often the direct consequence of interference with the normal process of free trade.

In the United Kingdom the conservative government, which carried out massive programs of "privatization" during the 1980s, argues that great benefits have followed. One thing, however, is becoming clear. The mere transfer of ownership is not enough. Exchanging a public monopoly for a private monopoly will not do the trick. There must be real competition.

---

*This is an attempt to regulate supply and price, rather than allow market forces to decide.

LEVEL FIVE: INTERNATIONAL COMPETITION

Imagine a country in which only one manufacturer built refrigerators and imports were prohibited. If someone wanted a refrigerator, the person could buy only from one product line. There is little doubt that products would meet only minimum standards for design and performance. Without a competing alternative, products of minimal efficiency are acceptable.

The western industrial tradition is inherently competitive. Consider the direction of personal computer development in recent years. There has been an explosion of invention and initiative as competing computer manufacturers leapfrog one another in their attempts to reap the harvest. Only those who are most innovative, cost effective, and fast to act will survive. The consumer benefits from free choice. Another illustration of this principle is the vast differences between the quality of Russian and Western-European cars. Freedom of choice requires that European motor manufacturers continually struggle to keep ahead. This is not true in the Eastern Block, where the consumer puts up with ill-designed and inefficient products. In the U.K. the customer usually suffers when the state creates a monopoly. The success of the oil industry in profitably exploiting natural resources is an excellent case history of the benefits of competition. Since oil companies compete with sharp claws, we all benefit.

Our belief is that the whole world benefits when competition operates freely. As the world becomes more and more one marketplace, competitiveness within one nation is insufficient. An organization must be as good as similar concerns anywhere else in the world; otherwise, security is an illusion. We live in an increasing global economy, and many economic and social problems are the direct result of the inability to compete on an international level. There can be no long-term solution to economic problems without a competitive edge.

People like competition, but only if they have a chance to win. Samantha Francis, daughter of one of the authors, is a student who said in conversation one day, "I believe in competition. I've never wanted to win for the sake of winning, but I am always happy to have someone to compete with. It brings the best out in me." We could say it no better.

SUMMARY: CORE PRINCIPLES — SURVIVAL OF THE FITTEST

- Lack of competition damages people, organizations, and nations.
- Competition is natural to human beings.
- Managers should learn more about the constructive use of competition as a motivator.
- Winning is a learnable set of skills.
- Not all competition is productive.
- Competition is not an end in itself, but a tool to be used.
- Competition between individuals can be a powerful motivator but can also be counterproductive.
- Managers should aim to make *all* employees into winners.
- People gain from competing against standards.
- Accountants should be encouraged to provide competitive data.
- Intercompany competitiveness is crucial to overall effectiveness.
- Nations succeed economically only if they are internationally competitive.

FIVE PRACTICAL STEPS TO ENCOURAGE COMPETITION

1. All individuals should be assessed to evaluate how far their work comes up to the highest standards. Find ways of stimulating individuals to compete with themselves (like athletes). Institute regular (perhaps quarterly) self-improvement counseling sessions in which managers give each employee individual performance data and discuss how improvements can be made.

2. Teams tackling similar tasks are often motivated by competition. Identify teams with which this would be useful and provide up-to-date information so that competitive performance can be judged. Advise managers and supervisors to encourage competition. Reward winners.

3. Undertake a project to identify unconstructive uses of the competitive principle. When destructive factors are uncovered, these should be remedied by redefining objectives to make it clear who the real enemy is.

4. Ask the accounting group to reexamine the data they produce and report on how this can be better used to promote competition within the organization.

5. Establish a newsletter which gives up-to-date information on the performance of your organization compared to your competitors. Buy examples of their products and have them carefully analyzed. Ensure that all of your employees know the strengths of the opposition.

REERENCES

1. See review in *London Sunday Times*, January 17, 1986, p. 1.
2. *Guidelines for Directors 1982*. (1982). London: The Institute of Directors, p. 15.
3. Darwin, C. (1982). *On the Origin of Species*. Burrow, J. W. (Ed.). London: Penguin Books.

C H A P T E R 15

Opportunism: Who Dares Wins

Despite the most brilliant planning, it is inevitable that unexpected opportunities and threats will occur. An organization cannot afford to ignore the unexpected. It is wiser actively to seek out new opportunities than to allow others, more fleet of foot, to grab the best chances. Opportunities have to be seized quickly, even though this may involve risks. The successful organization is a committed opportunist. It adopts this value: *Who dares wins*.

A group of managers can be held spellbound by listening to an outstandingly successful achiever describe his or her commercial adventures. Managers are thrilled by tales of challenge and success which cause the adrenaline to flow.

The folklore of business is laden with tales of managers who saw an opportunity, pounced on it, and turned an outside possibility into a commercial bonanza. This is an act of opportunism. Successful entrepreneurs are committed to acquiring the skills and willpower to seize and exploit opportunities.

Opportunists have a special view of the world; they perceive it to be vastly complex, turbulent, and continuously changing in unpredictable ways. "Constant change is here to stay" and rewards those who dare to win. In volatile environments there is much that can be planned, but there are always unpredictable elements which offer rich pickings for opportunists who develop a zest for detecting and rapidly exploiting attractive possibilities.

Opportunism is more than an quality; it is a cultural phenomenon within organizations and communities. For example, a primary reason for the inadequate performance of British industry in recent decades was that its managers failed to be successful opportunists. In the eighteenth and nineteenth centuries the capacity of British industry to be creative exploiters was world-renowned. Prior to 1939 one third of the world was under British influence. A decade or two later, the United Kingdom was being described as a spent force drifting from economic mediocrity into terminal decline. There are now hopeful signs of a renaissance of opportunism in management, as different economic policies revive latent opportunists. Opportunism is not simply creativity. Innovation itself abounds in Britain. A 1987 survey by Japan's Ministry for International Trade shows that over 55 percent of the "significant" inventions since World War II have been British, which is more than any other country including the United States (22 percent) and Japan (6 percent). Britain's problem has been an inability to harvest successfully the rich field of opportunities and innovative ideas. This joke illustrates the point: It is said that a Russian pilot defected to Japan with the latest MIG fighter. The next day the Russian authorities asked to have their airplane back. The Japanese replied: "Yes, of course, how many would you like?"

Adam Smith was correct when he said that people best help the public good by looking after themselves. An "enterprise culture" requires that people are rewarded for achievement rather than for having needs.

We have only to look around to see that opportunism is everywhere. Perhaps the largest group of successful opportunists in the United Kingdom over the past twenty years are shopkeepers of Indian descent who saw that small retail businesses were missing much potential trade. They changed the rules and captured business. Today there are few areas without Asian-run stores that thrive because they offer a wanted service. Opportunities always exist, even in the least promising circumstances.

Individual inspiration is the first stage of opportunism, but there is more to it than that. The need must be real, and the opportunist capable. Then a vision of a better future can be formed.

One of the most innovative thinkers of management of the post-war era, Edward de Bono, felt so strongly about exploiting opportunities that he wrote a book[1] about the subject. He says, "An opportunity is as real an ingredient in business as raw material, labour or finance — but it only exists when you see it." The author goes on to tell a personal story of the time when he wanted to build a raised platform in his apartment. He obtained various expensive quotations, some of which involved a four-month delay. Then came inspiration! He invited an exhibition contractor to construct the platform, which was done within 24 hours for half the conventional builder's cost. That was opportunism in action.

Opportunism is more than a management technique; it is a philosophy of life. We know of a non-Jewish friend who asks for Kosher food whenever he flies. Why? Because Kosher food is specially prepared on airlines, our friend gets an individual meal rather than a mass-produced concoction. Some years ago Gerald Francis, son of one of the authors, realized that the children in his school class became ravenous about midday. Quite unknown to his parents, he would buy a stock of sweets on his way to school. As the children reached the peak of hunger, Gerald sold his sweets for triple their cost. He frequently doubled his pocket money this way, even negotiating "trade" discounts with a shopkeeper for buying in quantity. In the summer he dealt in "ice pops," keeping them frozen in a special bag. Interestingly, this business lasted for only two years. Gerald had to seek new opportunities, saying "as the kids grew up, they got wiser, so I had to think of new ways to make money."

Such illustrations abound. Tourists in southern Italy can see a fine example of opportunism if they walk to the crater of Mt. Vesuvius. There is a small cafe just before the final lava-strewn path. As tourists realize the steepness of the route, they then pass a lady who is watching for flimsy footwear. When a poorly shod tourist passes, the opportunist grasps the victim by the shoulder and says, "Shoes no good for walk. Hire shoes here, only 1000 lira." Many tourists are whisked into the cafe to emerge in shoes lined with plastic. The story is not over! The descent is dusty and as weary tourists pass the same cafe, the opportunist stands by a collection of shoe brushes and a saucer for tips. She got our "Opportunist of the Month" award!

Such stories have one thing in common: they are full of life and vitality, as well as risk. Opportunism is a stance towards life which is inherently exciting. It is a fulfillment of a basic characteristic of the human spirit. No theory of motivation would be complete without it.

INDIVIDUAL OPPORTUNISM

Opportunistic individuals have learned to think in particular ways, having made a personal decision not to drift along passively in life. The opportunist maintains an inquisitive sense of detached observation, watching events unfold which inevitably provide opportunities. These can then be either exploited or avoided, depending on the wisdom of the opportunist and the potential payoff for success.

There is also much to be learned about the nature of opportunism by examining the biographies of successful people from any walk of life. Outstanding careers are always a good fit between personal motives and what the world has to offer. A career is each person's adventure and requires personal opportunism. The person who passively waits to be recognized is adopting a strategy with a high risk of failure. Effective opportunists take initiatives to make good things happen for themselves. They find new, often unexpected, possibilities that can be exploited.

Opportunism requires definite personal attributes that have been shown by Richard Boyatzis[2] to be key competencies in success at top management levels. Boyatzis has found in his research that three attributes are fundamental. He calls them "Efficiency Orientation," "Proactivity," and "Diagnostic Use of Concepts," which are, in our opinion, the essence of opportunism. Don't be put off by the jargon. These ideas have real merit.

First, "Efficiency Orientation" describes someone who wishes to do things better—perhaps better than the person has done previously, better than anyone else, or better than a standard. The individual who has high efficiency orientation thinks in terms of standards, measurements, and accomplishment. He or she is innovative and has highly developed skills in goal setting, planning, and organizing. People with this competence can be recognized because they:

- Set challenging but realistic targets
- Take moderate risks
- Measure their accomplishments
- Have clearly describable inner work standards
- State their standards clearly
- Write plans and review them
- Identify specific actions to be taken
- Organize resources (money/time/people, etc.)
- Talk about "return on investment," "reward for effort," etc.
- Watch for slippage of standards

Proactivity describes a disposition towards taking action and accomplishing something. Activity is purposefully instigated. The proactive person sees himself or herself as the originator of actions in life. People with this competence can be recognized because they

- See life and describe it in terms of taking action
- Feel (and state) that they are the agents of change
- Feel "master" of their own lives
- Feel "in control" of their own lives
- Initiate events (communication, proposals, meetings, etc.)
- Possess skills in information seeking and problem solving
- Often take the first step
- Take multiple steps to circumvent actual or potential obstacles
- Develop relationships with providers of information
- Accept responsibility for their own failures

The third opportunistic competence is "Diagnostic Use of Concepts." This describes an approach to thinking in which the opportunist detects meaningful patterns in information. He or she organizes, categorizes, and interprets events. Information is systematically tested against concepts. This way of thinking is deductive. Analytical and scientific approaches are valued. People who are able to use concepts to diagnose situations can be recognized because they

- Have models or theories to interpret events
- Build models/theories to explain new events
- Generalize from specific incidents to aid understanding
- Ask for "road maps" before they begin a project
- Apply theories of influencing to persuade others to go along with their views
- Perceive cues which tell them that a new set of concepts is necessary

- Sort out irrelevant information
- Categorize information in terms of whether it is critical, important or urgent

These three competencies provide a structured definition of opportunism. Although such attributes are difficult to teach, they can be learned. Developing individual opportunism is aided by the intentional application of the special thought processes and behaviors described. Our studies of opportunists have helped us identify eight distinctive characteristics that they seem to share:

- They are aware of what is going on around them.
- They know clearly what they like and what they want.
- They seek to get the best available in any situation.
- They do not allow themselves to get overfatigued. (Tiredness blunts opportunism.)
- They learn to do two things at once (like exercising on a stationary bicycle while watching television).
- They practice seizing opportunities even when it doesn't really matter. (Getting the best table in each restaurant they enter.)
- They give themselves a reward whenever they successfully exploit an opportunity.
- They mix with others who have developed the skills of identifying and seizing opportunities.

Opportunism requires an investment of thinking time. The manager must be willing to raise his or her head from immediate preoccupations or short-term achievements to consider a possibly better future. Speculation is an essential indulgence for the opportunist. The opportunist is wary of being kept constantly busy as this diminishes time for thought. The effective opportunist will be willing to be a business heretic but will always try to reduce the risks of failure. This process, which has been described as "proactive conservatism," is the essence of individual opportunism.

ORGANIZATIONAL OPPORTUNISM

Increasingly, organizations are advocating opportunism as a way of life. In the past few years even the mighty IBM has reorganized itself to become less monolithic. Of course, organizations cannot be opportunistic themselves, but they can create a climate in which individual opportunism flourishes. This requires that flexible structures must replace overcentralized decision making and red tape. The world is a volatile and changing place, so the unpredictable will occur and opportunities arise when they are least expected. The opportunist organization is poised to take advantage of such serendipity. One chief executive wanted her company to be "like a wild animal with its ears cocked and nose sniffing the air." Organizational opportunism begins with well-honed techniques for scanning the environment. The sagacious organization not only exploits accidents of fortune but also creates opportunities. A managing director told us, "as the world becomes more competitive, organizations must be opportunistic or they risk bankruptcy. That's it. Simple as that."

Ironically, some efforts to professionalize management have unintentionally undermined opportunism. Consider what happens in many large organizations when annual plans are prepared. The groundwork for this highly analytical procedure begins months before "Presentation Day." Environments are scanned, risks measured, and options studiously evaluated. The strong image of managers requires a coherent and logical plan written to high intellectual standards. Senior managers often hire business-school graduates to operate as planning specialists. Then months go by while plans are proposed, revised, and re-presented. When finally agreed on, strategy documents are likely to have most opportunistic elements removed. One director told us with great feeling that "rational long-term planning has destroyed the capacity to manage by the seats of our pants. The technocrats have the power, and it's a dangerous situation." Slowly, attempts to improve strategic-planning systems to promote opportunism are being introduced, and opportunist managers encourage trends away from worshipping only the gods of rationality and predictability.

In addition to the antiopportunistic bias of many corporate planning systems, there is another potential barrier to effective corporate opportunism. Those who are promoted to powerful roles often gain their high status through being excellent underlings. Such people are masters of their specializations. They administer supremely well, devise superb systems, but are naturally orientated towards safety and continuity. In our experience, successful organizations try to counter built-in risk avoidance by working hard to give individuals with entrepreneurial flair room to breathe. This builds a dynamic into top management, because opportunistic people dare to win.

Inspired change is rarely derived from conventional assumptions. What is needed is one person with a vision of a better future and the willpower to push through innovative ideas. This individual is a "product champion." The word *champion*: it means "one who fights for any cause. One who has defeated all opponents in any trial of strength or skill, and is open to contend with any new competitor" (Shorter Oxford Dictionary). Opportunism is a characteristic of individual champions, and systems should permit champions to emerge. This process is seen in the continuing emergence of small businesses, which do not have the wealth of larger, well-established concerns, but which are fueled by individuals with the willpower and the preparedness to seize an opportunity.

Large organizations must work hard to avoid acquiring an inertia that inhibits opportunism. Today enterprises cannot afford to wait for individuals to champion bright ideas; top management must structure opportunism. Historically, many organizations contained new ideas which were killed off by uninterested middle management. Many senior managers are rewarded for maintaining control and limiting waste; while this is essential, the organization must avoid eliminating opportunism simply because it seems untidy.

It is possible to reorient an organization towards a greater appreciation of economic factors. Companies like the Dow Chemical group have instituted a deliberate policy to rebuild a corporate culture based on commercial criteria. Steps that Dow undertook include these:

- Asking the question in performance reviews, "What have you done that's new?"
- Putting an evangelistic but practical top manager in charge of "debureaucratizing"
- Being prepared to act unconventionally
- Forming a high-level action group to push practical innovation
- Ensuring that new ideas are identified by a "technological gatekeeper"
- Telling, selling, and persuading people that changes are essential by presenting well-argued cases
- Convincing managers that if they are not part of the solution, they are part of the problem
- Truthfully answering questions from skeptics in order to build credibility
- Reorganizing to make new resources available for development
- Bringing development specialists close to the marketplace
- Removing excessive hierarchies to speed decision making
- Identifying and removing communication "blockages"
- Having an independently funded entrepreneurial department
- Providing facilities to incubate new projects
- Making beachhead acquisitions to gain footholds in new technologies
- Fighting the tendency by bureaucracy to overwhelm new acquisitions

Edward de Bono suggests that companies should structure opportunity seeking by instituting regular "opportunity audits."

Each executive is encouraged to examine regularly his or her "opportunity space." At the corporate level, "opportunity teams" coordinate the search for promising new ideas. The author points out that large company executives are trained to solve problems as they arise rather than to seize opportunities. This is an "opportunity-negative structure." Edward de Bono echoes our own theme when he writes, "The words 'opportunity' and 'opportunist' have had connotations. They suggest a hovering vulture rather than a hovering eagle . . . The opposite of opportunity-seeking is not stability or conservatism, it is stagnation and atrophy."

An interesting illustration of the vital importance of organizational opportunism is shown by the fortunes of the British telecommunications industry. For many years their products were dictated by a conventional post office. Although standards were rigorous, the level of innovation was low. In the late 1970s "de-regulation" opened doors to radical new products. Equipment from foreign suppliers began to compete with British manufacturers. This situation forced a revolution in the organization of telecommunication equipment companies which, for the first time, had to establish marketing departments and study consumers. It became imperative that a creative, flexible, and consumer-orientated philosophy permeated from top to bottom. One of the authors was privileged to be a consultant to a telecommunication-equipment manufacturer; he observed the creaks and groans as a total organization changed its structure, culture, and technology from old-style bureaucracy to emerge bursting with opportunism.

Organizational opportunism is correctly described as entrepreneurial. The original meaning of the word *entrepreneur* is "a person who stages dramas." Later the word became associated with commercial opportunists who seize possibilities which others fail to perceive or exploit. The entrepreneur is most definitely not an obedient functionary and so has difficulty fitting into centralized bureaucracies. Entrepreneurship tends to be better developed in small businesses; the market stall-holder or scrap-metal merchant is more likely to be a highly skilled opportunist than a system-bound middle manager in a large organization.

Successful organizational opportunism can be encouraged by the following:

- Top management wholeheartedly committed to successful innovation
- A culture which encourages opportunism by showing that venturesomeness is valued
- Training for managers in skills of managing innovation
- Creating mixed teams of developers and implementors to exploit ideas
- Offering tangible rewards and power to acknowledged innovators
- Allowing product champions room to grow
- Supporting entrepreneurial nurseries which allow risky but limited projects to flourish for a time
- Mentoring by experienced opportunists to transfer their attitudes and skills to more junior talent
- Devising imaginative suggestion schemes which collect ideas from large numbers of people
- Providing mechanisms that carefully evaluate ideas
- Identifying and exploiting sources of venture finance which assist opportunistic projects to get off the ground
- Maintaining overall commercial strength to enable resources to be available for entrepreneurial ventures
- Becoming highly skilled at evaluating potential markets for new ideas
- Being prepared to tolerate unconventional behavior from successful opportunists

Encouraging opportunism is a primary duty of management. The structure of organizations means that those at the top are in an extraordinarily privileged position. Only they can exploit major opportunities. Those working in subordinate roles are dependent on the opportunism of top managers. Managers, therefore, should accept that they have a moral obligation to be opportunistic. Only by seeking possible avenues for success or profit can they provide the positive leadership that their employees properly demand. In this context, employee or trade-union pressure can provide a useful stimulus. To illustrate, an electrical manufacturer decided to abandon an obsolete product and make three hundred people redundant. The trade union pushed managers by asking, "What have you done to find other products to replace the redundant line?" Management recognized that they had not fully considered the opportunities and were pressured into making a full study. The result was a range of new products that actually increased employment and business profitability. Opportunism thrives when we are "a little bit hungry."

POSTSCRIPT

Whilst this chapter was being prepared, by a strange coincidence, there was an amusing illustration of the principle. One of the authors was jogging in Richmond Park mulling over the concept of opportunism, and on his return discovered that he had mislaid his watch. After carefully thinking through the sequence of the jog, he became certain that the watch had been lost at the end where the final stretching and bending phase occurred. A search beneath the trees revealed nothing. But, as luck would have it, the watch alarm was set. Next morning, at five to seven, the jogging author was standing in his exercise spot. From a nearby tree a bird chirped but this was insufficient to drown a plaintive electronic beep coming from a clump of grass. Your author reacted like a young gun dog, going from hummock to hummock, knowing that the alarm would switch itself off in a few seconds. Fortunately, the watch was found and he learned, once again, that opportunism isn't just a principle of management—it is a practical philosophy for everyday life.

SUMMARY: CORE PRINCIPLES — WHO DARES WINS

- The world can never be totally planned: opportunities always occur.
- Opportunism is more than a philosophy of management: it is a way of life.
- Although many individuals can develop opportunistic attitudes and skills, they are not encouraged to do so in bureaucracies.
- If opportunism lacks a framework of principles, it can become a tool for immoral exploitation.
- To encourage opportunists, organizations can change their structures and cultures.
- Entrepreneurial skills are most naturally developed in small enterprises.
- Rigid strategic-planning procedures often inhibit opportunism.
- Some (but not all) top managers should be proven opportunists.
- Successful opportunists should be rewarded, both through recognition and material rewards.
- Unsuccessful opportunists also should be rewarded, with recognition and guidance (at least they tried!).
- It is essential to look outward at the environment (it is too easy to put all your effort into managing the status quo).
- Large companies should embrace a deliberate policy of encouraging opportunism.
- Pressure groups can be used to sharpen opportunistic thinking.

FIVE PRACTICAL STEPS TO ENCOURAGE OPPORTUNISM

1. Encourage individual opportunist skills through training programs that develop entrepreneurial competence. Ensure that these encourage self-awareness and put people into situations in which real opportunities exist. Tell your training department to prepare such a program. (Use de Bono's book on opportunities as a basic-reference in text.)

2. Review organization procedures, structures, and systems to determine whether potential opportunities are being lost through a surfeit of red tape.[3] Develop an experimental "fast track" to get ideas quickly into top decision-making teams. Set up a multidisciplinary task group to advise on how this can be accomplished.

3. Search for practical ways to reward opportunism at every level from director to shop-floor employees. Recognition, feedback, and encouragement should be used in addition to monetary gain. Tell your personnel director to review your reward policy with this fact in mind.

4. Look ahead for five to ten years in as much detail as possible (institutes like The Institute for the Future in Menlo Park, California can help). Conduct a very detailed analysis of the trends which are likely to affect your markets and technology. Hold senior management "teach-ins" to discuss potential opportunities. Establish a structure of "options teams" to explore opportunities. Progress many ideas at the same time. Ensure that the top team is kept in contact with the findings.

5. Set up opportunity panels with people from your organization and present or potential customers. Organize exchange sessions. Some firms estimate that 60 percent of good ideas can come this way. Ensure that the marketing director has this as an objective.

REFERENCES

1. de Bono, E. (1980). *Opportunities*. London: Penguin Books.
2. Boyatzis, R. (1982). *The Competent Manager: A Model for Effective Performance*. New York: John Wiley.
3. Woodcock, M., and Francis, D. (1989). *Unblocking Your Organization*. Aldershot, Surrey U.K.: Gower.

INDEX